Disclaimer Notice:

Please note the information contained within this document is for educational and entertainment purposes only. All effort has been executed to present accurate, up to date, reliable, complete information. No warranties of any kind are declared or implied. Readers acknowledge that the author is not engaged in the rendering of legal, financial, medical, or professional advice. The content within this book has been derived from various sources. Please consult a licensed professional before attempting any techniques outlined in this book.

CONTENTS

Introduction 4
CHAPTER 1. Starting Baking Bread 5
   Bread Basic Techniques 5
   Bread Making Methods 8
   Ingredients and Equipment 10
   Helpful Tips for Becoming a Professional/Most Common Mistakes and How to Avoid
   Them 14
CHAPTER 2. Recipes 16
Basic bread 16
   Classic Artisan Bread 16
   No – Knead Artisan Bread 17
   French Bread 18
   No – Knead Seeded Bread 20
   Cheese Bread 21
   Artisan Herb Bread 22
   Vegan Artisan Bread 23
   No – Knead Whole – Wheat Bread 24
   Harvest Grain Bread 25
   No – Knead Brioche Bread 26
   Oregano Garlic Bread 27
   Multigrain Bread 28
   Asiago Bread 30
   Rosemary Garlic Bread 32
   Artisan Rolls 33
   No – Knead Sandwich Bread 34
   Jalapeno Cheese Bread 35
Sourdough bread 36
   Sourdough Starter 36
   Gluten – Free Sourdough Starter 37
   Classic Sourdough Bread 38
   Artisan Sourdough Bread 39
   No – Knead Sourdough Bread 41
   Multigrain Sourdough Bread 43
   Rosemary Olive Sourdough Bread 44
   Gluten – Free Sourdough Bread 45
   French Sourdough Bread 46
   Sage and Caramelized Onion Bread 47
   Whole – Wheat Sourdough Bread 49
   Cinnamon Raisin Sourdough Bread 50
   Vegan Whole – Wheat Sourdough Bread 52
   Honey Wheat Sourdough Bread 53
Baguettes and Ciabattas 54
   Sourdough Baguette 54
   Classic French Baguette 55
   Whole – Wheat Baguette 57
   Gluten – Free French Baguette 58
   Alternative French Baguettes 59
   Seeded Pumpkin Baguette 61
   Wheat Shaft Baguette 62

Classic Ciabatta..63
No – Knead Ciabatta..65
Quick Ciabatta...66
Whole – Wheat Ciabatta..67
Pizza and Focaccia..69
Perfect Pizza Dough..69
No – Knead Pizza Dough..70
Vegan Pizza Dough..71
Neapolitan Pizza Crust...72
Artisan Margherita Pizza...73
Chicken Pesto Pizza..75
Hawaiian Pizza...76
Pizza Cubano...77
Extra Meat Pizza..78
Spicy Pepperoni Pizza..79
No – Knead Focaccia Bread...80
Rosemary Focaccia Bread..81
Cranberry and Goat Cheese Focaccia Bread...82
Sweet Tomatoes Focaccia..84
No – Knead Pistachios Focaccia...85
Apricot Prosciutto Focaccia..87
Focaccia Cheese Bread...88
Pastries and Biscuits..89
Crescent Rolls...89
Artisan Croissant Dough..90
Puff Pastry Dough..92
Apple, Bacon, and Caramelized Onion Turnovers...93
Flaky Rosemary Biscuits..94
Gluten – Free Buttermilk Biscuits...95
Fruit Almond Cruffins..96
Cherry Turnovers...97
Pastry Cinnamon Rolls...98
Homemade Soft Pretzel..99
Sweet Ricotta Pastries..100
Sporcamuss Pastries...102
Onion, Spinach, and Cheese Turnovers..103
French Apple Tart..104
Cream Peach Pie...106
Caramel Apple Pie...108

INTRODUCTION

An artisan is a person who makes distinctive, high – quality products in small quantities, usually by hand or using traditional methods, and as a noun, it pertains to an artisan or the product of an artisan. Its philosophy is wholly about quality over quantity, and it is something we miss in our mass – produced world.

"Faster, better, cheaper" is how most products are made nowadays, and while it's good for business, for consumers, it results in far from the best store shelves. Don't get me wrong – they're okay – they are affordable and obtainable, but sometimes we all want something nicer and more special.

The same is with bread. What we can found in our local groceries is okay. It's cheap, it's eatable, and it's not too unhealthy. But if you've ever tasted bread from a good dedicated bakery or even better – a home – baked one, you won't be fully satisfied with grocery bread ever again. In a few words, that's how and why I got into artisan bread baking, and that's what this book is about.

In this book, I've put all the knowledge and experience that I've gained from years of baking for my family and me. I'll give you the best recipes and advice I can, helping you to become a good or an even better baker.

I've tried to cover the topic of artisan breadmaking wholly, answering all the questions I could think of – from the most basic to the most advanced ones. And I hope that I've succeeded in all of that.

So, turn this page and check if I've accomplished that or not. Anyways, happy baking!

CHAPTER 1. STARTING BAKING BREAD
Bread Basic Techniques

The principles of bread baking have the same for thousands of years. The basic ingredients are water, yeast, salt, and flour.

All bread making processes rely on five key steps: mixing, proofing, kneading, shaping, and baking.

Mixing

These days electronic stand mixers with dough hooks are insanely popular. Many have said goodbye to the tough task of hand – operated mixing and switched to the modern technologies that make mixing and kneading dough much easier. And there's no shame in it whatsoever.

That said, it's still good to do this by hand sometimes. There are times in some recipes where a brief knead by hand is best, and there is also a lot to be said about understanding your dough by taking the time to work with it directly.

So, to mix the dough, pour some flour onto the into a bowl or worktop and form a medium crater in the center. Into this crater, add all of the wet ingredients – for example, water and yeast – along with the sourdough starter. Then sprinkle the salt just around the edge of the filled crater.

Using a wooden spoon, or the fingers of one hand, move in small circular motions to mix the wet ingredients and yeast together, gradually pulling in more and more flour from around the edge of the well. Increase the size of the circular motions and keep moving until you'll mix all the flour in. As a result, you'll have a very soft, sticky, messy lump.

Proofing

In bread baking terms, proving or proofing means to allow the dough to rise. The proof refers to the action of the yeast, that causes the dough to rise and creates that airy texture. In most of the basic bread recipes, the dough proofs or proves twice.

After continuously punching down, folding, kneading, and stretching your dough, you will get it ready for its final proof by forming it into its final shape.

Then put it into a basket, bowl, or bread pan, cover it with a towel, and perform a shorter second rise at room temperature. During this time, the loaf should nearly double in size.

Kneading

The reason kneading is such an important part of bread making is because it creates structure and strength in the dough, leaving it soft and silky with a subtle cushiony feel.

It takes no more than a just few minutes, requiring just your hands, a bit of flour, that you will use to keep the dough from sticking, and a flat surface.

The process would be easier if you use a tabletop or countertop that allows you to comfortably extend your arms to knead the dough without hunching over a table.

Start with generously sprinkling the surface with flour, then scrape the dough out of the bowl onto your preferred work surface

Begin kneading the dough by pushing it down and outward, mainly using heels of your palms. Fold the dough in half towards you and press down. Then, again, use the heels of your hands to push downwards and outwards, stretching and lengthening the dough fibers and strands of gluten.

Rotate the dough about 45 degrees and resume kneading in the same way as before. If it is getting too sticky, feel free to add a little more flour, and continue to knead, fold, and turn the dough, until it is supple and smooth.

To ensure that the dough has been kneaded enough, you can do perform a "windowpane" test. Tear off a small bit of dough and hold it between the first two fingers of each hand and your thumbs so the dough is right in front of you. Then, gently pull your thumbs and other fingers away from each other to stretch the dough out. If the dough doesn't break, you've kneaded it enough; if the membrane pulls apart, you need to knead it a bit more.

Shaping

At first glance, it's obvious that shaping is used to impart a certain look and aesthetic to a dough. However, it's more than that: it dictates how we slice, eat, and, ultimately, share the bread we bake. Starting with the same dough, we can create drastically different results simply by shaping it differently.

Bread can be formed into almost any shape and form you want, but it always affects its qualities. Some bread comes out better in a traditional loaf pan shape, while others, like sourdough, are nice as a round loaf as well.

Still, shaping is mostly a personal preference, but there is a basic technique for forming the traditional rectangular loaf of bread.

You will need a clean counter or/and board, rolling pin, bread pan, bread dough, flour, and butter or cooking spray.

Starting with a good rested dough round, flip it onto your floured work space and spread it out gently.

Make "two wings", by pulling both bottom two sides away from each other.

Fold the left side over to the middle and the right to the middle over the left.

Pull the top of the "envelope" using both hands up and away, then fold it over and down to the middle, sealing upon the dough.

Using both hands, just grab the bottom and pull up and over straight to the top.

Using both hands again, tuck the dough and drag it down towards your body creating tension around the outside of the dough. After each drag you make, spin the dough 180 degrees on the work surface and continue the same dragging until the dough becomes uniform in shape and the outside of the loaf becomes smooth without any tears or bulges.

Using your bench knife or other handy tool, flip the dough and place it in the proofing basket with the seam facing up.

If you think that your dough is excessively slack and weak after the shaping, you can add a little more structure to the dough by pinching its top.

After you let your dough rest for a few minutes in the proofing basket, fold the outside edge of the dough up over to the middle. Do this at each four sides, where the flaps are opposite the other flaps, to create a small "package".

After you do the four folds, you'll end up with a tighter boule. This final pinching will create that missing amount of tension in the dough, adding strength to a boule that otherwise might spread significantly in the oven.

Baking

There are probably a thousand and more oven types and models, that are all built and behave differently. Therefore, you should always use the temperatures and times mentioned in our recipes and all others as nothing more than just indications, always adjusting them to the particular properties of your exact oven to get the best results.

Your oven can make or break your painstakingly prepared loaves, so it is wise to know the sometimes – quirky traits of your oven.

Firstly, it is important to detect what the real temperature of your oven is compared to the temperature indicated in the settings. You can easily do this using a 'true temp' oven thermometer.

The closer your bread is to the top of your oven, the faster heat gets transferred, which means quicker browning and potential burning!

It's worth noting that if your heating system is located too close to where your bread bakes, the top can burn. To prevent that from happening, you have to adjust the temperature or make sure that you just lower your oven temp after about 10 minutes, so the spirals stop burning.

Introduce steam inside your oven to allow the dough to grow at the start of the baking process. The moisture keeps the outside gelatinous and moist, so while the inside of your bread tries to expand under the heat, it is not hold by a dried out outer shell. This is known as oven spring.

One regularly used method is to have a tray in the oven, put bread in the oven, pour the hot water onto the tray, and then quickly close the door so the steam is trapped.

If you are for some reason not happy with the baking results, you can try to create an 'oven in an oven' by using a cast iron pan or a cloche, if your oven can hold this. The roof of the pan or cloche traps moisture rising from the dough and forms the steam that produces a crusty loaf with a creamy crumb. Make sure you preheat the oven and pan together.

Bread Making Methods

When I was just getting into bread baking, I came across a lot of diverse methods and techniques that got me confused. But over time I have tried many, and here is the summary of all the bread making methods that I know about for your understanding and easy reference.

Direct Dough/Straight Dough

This method is basic and it's one of the easiest for making bread. A first – time baker should start with this to grasp the process before proceeding to other, more advanced methods.

In this method, all of the ingredients are directly mixed, and then kneaded together. After the kneading is complete, the dough is left to proof for about 60+ – minutes or until it doubles in size. This is followed by shaping and a second "round" of proofing before baking.

Starter Dough/Pre – Fermented Dough

This is a dough where a starter part is mixed separately and left to ferment for some period of time before being added to the bread dough. The purpose of it all is to get a better aroma and flavor thanks to the higher production of alcohol, carbon dioxide, and enzymes during the fermentation. The dough is also more mature and hydrated, hence the bread is softer.

There are few main pre – ferment dough methods: Biga, Poolish, Pate Fermentee/Old Dough, Sponge Dough, and Madre Bianca.

Biga Method

Biga is a traditional Italian low hydration method. It takes longer to finish the fermentation if compared with Poolish Dough, that contains the same amount of yeast.

The Biga starter uses 25 – 50% of the total flour from the recipe.

Dough ratio of flour to water is 100:55%

Dough uses the amount of yeast that equals to 0.25 – 1% of the total flour. The longer the time of fermentation is, the less that yeast is required.

Ferment at room temperature for 15 – 18 hours or in the fridge for up to 3 days.

The method is often used for Ciabatta, Focaccia, and Italian bread.

Poolish Method

This technique was developed by Polish bakers in Vienna, and was later adopted by French bakers, according to some articles. Poolish is highly hydrated, wet dough.

The Poolish starter uses 25% – 50% of the total flour from the recipe.

Dough ratio of flour to water is 100:100%

Dough uses the amount of yeast that equals to 0.25 – 1% of the total flour. The longer the time of fermentation is, the less yeast that is required.

Ferment at room temperature for 15 – 18 hours or in the fridge for up to 3 days.

Often used for Country loaves, Baguettes, and other crusty breads.

Pate Fermentee/Old Dough Method

Traditionally, bread makers took a portion (usually around ⅓) of the bread dough and saved it overnight for baking tomorrow. That's why sometimes it's also called "Old Dough". But if you don't bake every day, you can still make it from scratch.
The Old Dough starter uses 25% – 50% of the total flour from the recipe.
Dough ratio of flour to water is 100:60%
Dough uses the amount of yeast that equals to 0.25 – 1% of the total flour.
3 – 4% of the total ingredient mass is salt and sugar.
Ferment at room temperature for 12 – 16 hours or in the fridge for 24 – 36 hours.
Can be used for almost anything.

Sponge Dough Method

The Sponge Dough is popular in America, some parts of Asia, and Central Europe. It produces bread with a soft crumb, unique aroma, and better shelf – life.
The Sponge Dough starter uses 60 – 80% of the total flour from the recipe.
Dough ratio of flour to water is 100:60%
Dough uses the amount of yeast that equals to 1 – 5% of the total flour.
Ferment at room temperature for 2 – 8 hours or until there are plenty of bubbles on the surface.
Often used for sweet breads/enriched breads or breads that don't need more structure.

Pre – Cooked Dough

There **Yudane** vs. **Tangzhong** (Water Roux) Method
Both Tangzhong and Yudane use the method of cooking a small percentage of the flour and liquid (milk or water) very briefly before combining the resulting thick slurry with the remaining ingredients. Cooking the flour makes the starch gelatinize. This makes the texture of the bread fluffy and soft.
According to some articles, Yudane was invented by Mr. Saito of a flour company from Japan, while Tangzhong is a Chinese method.

Yudane Method

When you make bread using this method, it stays soft and fresh for longer than most other ordinary homemade bread. It is because of the lactobacilli bacteria fermentation.
The starter uses 20% of the total flour in the recipe.
Dough ratio of flour and water is 1:1
Boiling water is needed to scald the flour (so you don't need to cook it over the fire).
The scalded dough can only be used at least 4 hours later or overnight in the fridge.

Tangzhong Method

The dough uses 7% of the total flour in the recipe.
Dough ratio of flour and water = 1:5
The dough is cooked under low fire until it thickens to a glue – like texture.
The cooked dough can be used once it's cooled down, or you can also store it overnight in the fridge.

Ingredients and Equipment

Ingredients

When you want to try something new, you always need to find some info about how to do it and what can help you to do it better. In our case, it's artisan bread making! I tried to fill this subchapter with all of the essential info and details that will help you in the beginning. You will know what ingredients you need to always keep in your kitchen and what equipment works best for you!

Flour

Flour is the most essential ingredient for bread making. Without flour and its ability to create the gluten, the bread you have baked won't acquire the right structure because flour is the key component that brings the rest of the ingredients together.

If you are the beginner, I recommend starting your breadmaking with simple recipes based on all – purpose flour. After you have had some practice and understood how it works, you won't be afraid to experiment with more specialized flour such as whole wheat flour, bread flour, rice flour, or gluten – free. Also, you can use other flour based on nuts (almond flour), fruits, legumes, coconut or grains like quinoa flour.

Yeast

Yeast is as essential for breadmaking as flour is. The main function of yeast is rising your dough and giving it the amazing taste and aroma that makes your homemade bread so delicious. In combination with the other ingredients added to finish the reactions, yeast helps to bake a perfectly done loaf of hot, fresh, and crusty homemade bread.

Every yeast package contains thousands of living microorganisms. Activate them with warm liquids and feed with starch or sugar, and then the yeast starts to release small bubbles of carbon dioxide gas. That's the main reason why your dough rises and gets this light texture after you take it out of the oven.

Fat

The main source of fat for bread making is butter, but oils also can be used to enrich your dough with fat – it's all depends on the recipe.

If you want to give your bread an interesting flavor, use olive oil, but only a good quality one. If you don't, it will taste bitter. Use sunflower or canola oil for a neutral taste, if you don't want any additional flavors in your bread.

Water

Water is an essential ingredient for mixing your dough because it does two main things:

Yeast dissolves and activates in warm water.

It helps all of the ingredients to come together in an elastic and sticky dough.

Milk, cream, buttermilk, or juice can be used to change the flavor or texture of the bread. Use only warm liquids when adding them to the dry ingredients because cold liquids will slow down the yeast action or even stop it. Too hot liquid will destroy the yeast and prevent it rising. So always try to use 100°F – 110°F warm water to avoid any problems while mixing.

Salt

Newbies may wonder why salt is also an essential ingredient for baking bread. Actually, it's important for your bread flavor. Salt affects the final taste by balancing and enhancing the flavor, but be careful with amount you add. Try to use a fine, thin salt for mixing your dough and flake or sea salt for serving if needed.

Sweetener

There are a several different types of ingredients that can be used as sweeteners:
 natural granulated or powdered sugar such as stevia or coconut sugar
 processed sugar, that can be found in powdered or granulated form
 liquid sweeteners such as maple syrup, honey, or agave syrup
Most recipes are based on a granulated white sugar. You may also find recipes that include liquid sweeteners such as malt, maple, or agave syrup, and especially honey.

Eggs

Eggs are also known as an essential baking ingredient. The egg yolk is used for binding liquids and fat by emulsifying and for bringing your cake. This makes the cake nice and light.

You will see that some recipes require you to separate the white from the yolk while others use the whole egg. It's better to use fresh good quality eggs if possible. For example, cage – free or free – range eggs.

Milk or Cream

Milk is really important in baking, as it's a kind of universal ingredient – it adds some fat, brings flavor and binds together all the ingredients to form a dough. There are no strict rules about milk, follow the recipe or use whatever milk you like, but it should be fresh. I prefer to add full cream milk that noticeably enriches my baking goods.

The most popular choice is dairy – milk – it's commonly used in the majority of recipes. If you can't use it for some reason, you can replace it with non – dairy milk such as coconut or almond milk. They will bring a subtle flavor to your bread.

Chocolate and Cacao Powder

I haven't met a person who doesn't like a chocolate yet. Other than fruit, it is the most popular ingredient for sweet baked goods and desserts. Each recipe requires either cacao powder or cooking chocolate.

There is a difference between their use – you need to melt cooking chocolate before using it, while cacao powder is a dry ingredient. I highly recommend you find good quality cacao powder and chocolate, you will discover how much better your baking tastes. If you want a less sweet taste, then use dark cooking chocolate or unsweetened cacao powder.

Spices and Flavoring Extracts

The easiest way to make a flavored bread is adding spices! For savory bread I commonly use rosemary, oregano, turmeric, garlic, sage, nutmeg, and black pepper, etc. For example, rosemary and oregano go well with cheese, tomato, or garlic bread. If you are thinking about what spices you could add to your sweet baking, then you should consider cinnamon, ground cloves, ginger, star anise, and many types of flavor extracts such as coffee, vanilla, or almond extract.

Other toppings

Fruits, vegetables, and things like cheese can be also used as a topping for your bread, cakes, and other pastries. For savory bread we often use olives, jalapeno peppers, spinach, onion, tomatoes (for focaccia), cheese, or bacon. It all can be added along with spices. For the sweet baking, use different berries, and fresh and dried fruits.

You can make an amazing filling for your pastry by combining your favorite ingredients. I have prepared some delicious and easy recipes for this occasion! See the Pastry and Biscuits recipe section if you want to try something new or don't have a nice bakery in your town.

Equipment

In baking, your choice of equipment can lead to either a satisfying result or disappointing failure. Thankfully, the modern market offers tons of products that help to perform different baking tasks — anything from measuring and mixing to decorating and finishing.

Here are some of the most basic tools you might come across:

Measuring Equipment

Measuring spoons and cups. Proportions are crucial for any baking recipe, so measuring spoons and cups are irreplaceable for both professional and amateur bakers. Measuring cups are great for measuring liquids, and spoons are ideal for scooping dry ingredients.

Digital Scales. For dry ingredients, a digital scale is definitely the most accurate way to measure. The level of flour in one cup can change up to 30 percent depending on whether it's been sifted or not, how you poured flour into the measuring cup, and what the humidity level is that day. Precise measuring can make the difference between heavy bricks and airy treats.

Mixing Equipment

Strainer or Sifter. Nothing is worse than getting a clump of baking soda or flour when biting into a slice of cake, and sifting can easily prevent that from happening. A sifter is an inexpensive and vital piece of equipment that can be useful for almost any recipe.

Bowls. It's best to use bowls that are made of a nonreactive metal (e.g., stainless steel) or glass. Plastic bowls can retain tastes and flavors that you might not want next time, and they are unsuitable for whisking egg yolks and sugar over a pot of simmering water, or melting chocolate.

Pastry Blender. This tool helps you to cut fat into dry ingredients to create flaky breads, crusts, and scores. If you don't want to do the manual work, the same result can be achieved with a food processor.

Silicone Spatula. If you do any baking at home, then you probably already own one of these. If not, it should be number one on your list. They're heat – resistant enough, they don't stain or absorb flavors, and they are essential for gently mixing things.

Whisk. A whisk is the best manual tool to thoroughly combine just about anything. Use an all – purpose whisk, or test your arm strength with an extra – wide balloon whisk when mixing everything up.

Stand Mixer. A stand mixer is sure to make your baking life much easier. Stand mixers can be a great investment in your cooking arsenal, making everything from whipping egg whites to kneading dough a breeze.

Portioning Equipment

Bench or Dough Scrape. As the name indicates, a bench scraper is for getting stuck – on ingredients off your workplace, but it can also be used for portioning. They can be made of either plastic or metal, with plastic being great for getting the last bits of dough or batter out of a mixing/proofing bowl.

Baking Equipment

Silicone Baking Mat. Made out of silicone and fiberglass, these nonstick mats are a great replacement for parchment paper, since they are reusable.

Bakeware. Getting at least one classically shaped loaf pan is a must for bread baking. Most bakeware can be made of metal, glass, or silicone. Glass lets you see how brown your baking is getting, metal is the best conductor of heat, and silicone takes away all worries about sticking.

Oven Thermometer. The most – critical factor a lot of home bakers tend to ignore is making sure you're actually baking at the same temperature as you think you are. An oven thermometer is a handy gadget to prevent mishaps caused by baking things at either too high or too low temperatures.

Finishing and Cooling Equipment

Timer. Though smell can help with indication of readiness, relying only on your nose can sometimes lead to failure. Set the timer before what the recipe calls for, just a few minutes in case the food is ready early.

Readiness Tester. Though a toothpick often does the job just fine, a metal tester has a few obvious advantages. First, it is reusable; second, its length makes it easier to use with thick baked goods, and third – it's just more convenient.

Baking Rack. The rack provides better air circulation to help speed up the chilling process and inhibit overcooking. It's saves that hard time waiting before you can taste your baking, so it's totally worth it.

LAST BUT NOT LEAST...

Oven. The heat source is located either at the bottom or the top of your oven, which creates hot and cold spots, so it's always best to bake on a rack that's placed in the middle. And if have a convection oven, it will gradually help to prevent uneven cooking, but be sure to either shorten the baking time by roughly a quarter for most recipes, or reduce the temperature by about 25°F.

Helpful Tips for Becoming a Professional/Most Common Mistakes and How to Avoid Them

If you are finally ready to start the exciting process of bread making with the first recipe, I recommend knowing what mistakes you should avoid to get the best result and advance your skills in the right direction. Don't be upset! We all make mistakes, and it's good – it's your chance to become a better cook! With these notes you will come closer to the level of professional baking. I hope they will help a lot during your whole bread baking journey.

Mistake #1: Don't over – flour your wet dough

People always feel uncomfortable with sticky dough, so they add more and more flour. And when it's ready, they end up with a very moist dough. If you want to make a good loaf of homemade bread, you get over it. Of course, the dough shouldn't be so sticky, it's great when it still lightly sticks to the sides of the bowl, but then easily pulls off. The more you bake, the more experience you get.

Mistake #2: I don't need a digital scale

Popular opinion – you don't need to use the scales for measuring your ingredients. People think that it's useless for them but the scales are one of the main helpers in the kitchen. For example, there is a huge difference between 1 teaspoon of kosher salt and 1 teaspoon of finely granulated. You always need to use the exact amount of ingredients mentioned in recipe. A wrong miss – scaled ratio – even of one ingredient – will change the texture and the taste of your bread. Always be careful with measuring.

Mistake #3: Not Making Notes

Try to keep notes about the results you got while baking a bread. Note what condition your crumb structure is in – is it too loose or too dense, are you satisfied with the crust, do you like the flavor? Be sure that your notes will make the further process of baking much easier because your last experience will help you to avoid mistakes or remind you of your best moves and ideas. Every professional always has a notebook with his/her notes in the kitchen.

Mistake #4: Doing your bread in a standing mixer

You can use a standing mixer while making the dough but don't overuse it! When a mixer does all the work for you, you can't expect to get a real artisan bread loaf. Remember that a mixing machine can dry out the bread, over – oxidize it and as a result you get a dry loaf. Using a machine is good option in the beginning, but the main key of artisan breadmaking is your hands. Feel your dough with your fingers and it will tell you everything.

Mistake #5: Switching up flours

Did you look at the recipe and decide to switch up its flour for another one? Think twice! Each flour may have its own protein level that affects the loftiness of your bread when take it out from the oven. For example, white flour is a little higher in protein the whole – grain flour. If you switch white flour for whole – grain, don't expect to see a puffy bread loaf. It will be a flat loaf due to whole grain bran cut through the proteins' gluten network. So, if you want to switch flours up, try to search different variations of the bread you want to be sure it won't spoil anything, and you get the desired result.

Mistake #6: My bread doesn't need to proof completely

Before going to the oven, you should let your dough have a final rest, or proof in other words. Yes, you may look forward to seeing what you have made, but for the best result you need to be more patient. Leave it to proof and then check if it's ready to go in the oven. Slightly poke the dough with your fingertip to make an indentation. If it's slowly creeping back and doesn't go back all the way, it's ready to bake!

Mistake #7: Taking your loaf out of the oven too early

Taking your bread out of the oven is a very important moment when you want to get a beautiful golden – brown crust. You will notice that there is a fine line between perfectly done and burned bread. There are two ways to check if the bread is ready and I recommend using both of them. The first one is the visual way: if you see crust is very firm, dry, has deep golden – brown color and some dark spots, – it's time to take it out! If you see the crust is pale, give your bread a few more minutes.

The second way is taking an internal temperature. Insert a thermometer (instant read) into middle of the loaf. If you don't want to leave any signs after checking, insert it at an angle through the bottom or side of the bread. Almost all breads are ready at 190°, those breads that are enriched with eggs, butter, or milk are done when the internal temperature is about 20

CHAPTER 2. RECIPES

BASIC BREAD

Classic Artisan Bread

SERVINGS: 1 PREP TIME: 15 min. + 18 h. COOK TIME: 45 min.

CARBS – 47 g FAT – 1 g PROTEIN – 7 g CALORIES – 22

Ingredients
- 3¼ cups all – purpose flour
- 1½ – 2 tsp kosher sea salt
- ½ tsp active dry yeast
- 1½ cups warm water

Directions
1. Mix the yeast, flour, and salt in a bowl. Gradually pour in the water, while stirring with a spoon. Stir well to incorporate. Mix the dough gently and form into a rough ball.
2. Put it into a large bowl and cover with a kitchen towel. Leave for 18 hours until doubled in size and covered with bubbles.
3. When it's done, preheat the oven to 450°F and place a closed Dutch oven into it for 30 minutes.
4. Flour the work surface and place the dough onto it. Form a ball by folding the corners underneath. Put the dough onto a large piece of parchment paper. Dust with flour, and cover again. Leave for 15 minutes.
5. Lightly brush the top with water to dampen the bread.
6. Take out the Dutch oven and transfer the bread into it by holding the corners of the parchment paper. Close and bake for 30 minutes.
7. Next, remove the lid and bake uncovered for 10 – 15 minutes to brown the top.
8. Carefully take it out from the oven and transfer the bread to a cooling rack.
9. Let it cool for 30 – 40 minutes before slicing and serving.

No – Knead Artisan Bread

SERVINGS: 1 PREP TIME: 2h. 15 min. + 1 day COOK TIME: 45 min.

CARBS – 48 g FAT – 1 g PROTEIN – 6 g CALORIES – 230

Ingredients

- *⅓ cup dairy – free yogurt*
- *1 Tbsp All – Natural Almond Butter*
- *¼ cup 100% Instant Oats*
- *½ cup almond milk*
- *1 pinch almonds, crushed*
- *1 tsp cinnamon*
- *1 pinch salt*

Directions

1. Put the yeast, flour, and salt into a large bowl and mix well. Pour in the liquids and add the herbs, mix well.
2. Cover with plastic wrap and leave for 1 day (at room temperature). The dough should rise and be covered with bubbles.
3. Flour the work surface and transfer the dough onto it. Dust it with flour.
4. Fold it in half, form a ball, stretching and tucking dough edges underneath the ball.
5. Generously flour a kitchen towel and place the ball onto it. Cover with another floured towel. Leave for 2 hours to rise.
6. Preheat the oven to 450°F. Place a closed Dutch oven into the oven to preheat.
7. Remove the Dutch oven from the oven. Open the lid and transfer the dough onto an ungreased baking dish seam – side up and shake it a little.
8. Close the lid and bake for 30 minutes.
9. Remove the lid and bake uncovered for 15 – 20 minutes until the crust is golden brown.
10. Let it cool on a rack for 30 – 40 minutes before slicing.
11. Slice and serve with dinner.

French Bread

SERVINGS: 1 PREP TIME: 1h. 30 min. COOK TIME: 45 min.

CARBS – 41 g FAT – 1 g PROTEIN – 6 g CALORIES – 197

Ingredients
- *3½ cups all – purpose flour + extra for dusting*
- *1¼ cups warm water*
- *2¼ tsp active dry yeast*
- *1 tsp sugar*
- *1½ tsp kosher salt*

Directions
1. Mix the yeast, water, and sugar in a large bowl. Then let it proof for 5 minutes.
2. Add the flour and salt to a bowl. Mix until the dough pulls off from the bowl sides and there are no dry bits.
3. Lightly flour each side of the dough to prevent sticking. Put it back in the bowl and turn it over. Cover using a towel, and leave for 1 hour.
4. When the dough has doubled in size, lightly flour the working surface.
5. Gently transfer the dough onto the floured surface.
6. Sprinkle flour across the dough top, then start shaping into a round loaf.
7. Pull every corner of the dough to the middle. Repeat until the dough is tight and resists your folds. Flip it over and press into a round loaf.
8. Flour a medium bowl and place the loaf inside (seam – side down). Cover and leave for 30 minutes.
9. Meanwhile, preheat the oven to 460°F and put an empty Dutch oven into it.
10. Take out the Dutch oven and lay it on your counter with parchment paper.
11. Carefully place your dough onto the parchment. The seam side should be up this time (for cracks on top of the bread).
12. Carefully lift up the bread and put it into the preheated Dutch oven by holding the parchment sides.

13. Using oven mitts, close the lid of the Dutch oven and put it back into the oven. Bake for 30 minutes.

14. Open the lid and bake for another 10 – 15 minutes, uncovered. It is done when the bread has a deep color and a nice brown crust.

15. Take it out from the oven and lift the bread by holding the corners of parchment paper out onto a cooling rack. Let the bread cool for 30 – 40 minutes.

16. Slice and serve.

No – Knead Seeded Bread

SERVINGS: 1 PREP TIME: 2 h. 10 min. + overnight COOK TIME: 1 h.

CARBS – 19 g FAT – 6 g PROTEIN – 3 g CALORIES – 207

Ingredients

- *2⅔ cups strong white bread flour, plus extra to dust*
- *1½ cups warm water*
- *1⅓ cups whole – meal bread flour*
- *¼ tsp fast – action dried yeast*
- *½ Tbsp fine sea salt*
- *½ cup mixed seeds*
- *1 handful raisins (optional)*
- *2 Tbsp clear honey*

Directions

1. Mix the yeast, flours, seeds, raisins, and salt in a large bowl. Create a well in the middle of the mixture.
2. Mix the water and honey in another bowl, then add it to the well. Using a wooden spoon, mix until it is a shaggy and sticky dough, don't leave any flour in a bowl. Cover and leave overnight.
3. The next day, the dough should be a little bubbly and wetter. Flour the working surface and transfer the batter onto it. Fold it twice. Cover with a bowl and leave for 15 minutes to rest.
4. Dust a piece of baking paper with flour.
5. Form a round dough and place onto the floured baking paper. Sprinkle with flour and cover with a bowl. Leave for 2 hours to double in size.
6. Preheat the oven to 430°F and place a Dutch oven (covered with a lid) into it for 30 minutes. When the bread has risen, make a crosshatch pattern on it with a sharp knife.
7. Take out the Dutch oven and carefully open the lid. Lift the dough up into hot oven, using the paper corners. Cover with the lid.
8. Bake for 30 minutes. Then, bake for 15 – 20 minutes uncovered to get a brown crust.
9. Remove and let it cool for 35 – 40 minutes before serving.

Cheese Bread

SERVINGS: 1 PREP TIME: 3 h. 30 min. COOK TIME: 50 min.
CARBS – 21 g FAT – 10 g PROTEIN – 5 g CALORIES – 196

Ingredients

- ½ cup buttermilk, warmed to 110°F
- ⅓ cup water, warmed to about 110°F
- 2 ¼ tsp active dry yeast
- 2 Tbsp granulated sugar
- 5 Tbsp unsalted butter, melted
- 1 large egg, at room temperature
- 2 cups shredded cheddar cheese
- 1 tsp salt
- ¾ tsp garlic powder
- 3 cups bread flour

Directions

1.   Add the buttermilk, water, yeast, and sugar into a stand mixer bowl (dough hook fitted), and mix. Cover and leave for 5 minutes.
2.   Add 1 cup of flour, butter, egg, garlic powder, and salt. Beat the mixture for 30 seconds at a low speed, then scrape down all of the sides of the bowl, add the rest of the flour. Then beat for 2 minutes more at a medium speed, the dough should pull away from bowl sides.
3.   Beat the dough for an additional 2 minutes.
4.   Grease a large bowl with oil. Transfer the dough into it and turn to coat all of the sides with oil. Cover with a kitchen towel and let it rise for 2 hours to double in size.
5.   Grease a loaf pan (9×5") and flour the work surface. Punch down the batter and place on the floured surface.
6.   Roll it out into a rectangle (9×15"). Cover with cheese all over (leave a ½" border uncovered).
7.   Tightly roll the dough into a 15" log. Place it on its seam. Shape the top of the bread with a pattern. Put it in the loaf pan and cover using a kitchen towel. Let it rest for 30 minutes.
8.   Set the oven rack to the lower third position. Preheat the oven to 350°F.
9.   Make a tent over the pan with foil and bake for 45 – 55 minutes. Remove from the oven and cool for 10 minutes in the pan, then remove from the pan and cool on a wire rack.

Artisan Herb Bread

SERVINGS: 1 PREP TIME: 10 min. + day COOK TIME: 30 min.

CARBS – 27 g FAT – 2 g PROTEIN – 5 g CALORIES – 143

Ingredients
- *3 ¼ cups all – purpose flour*
- *2 tsp coarse Kosher sea salt*
- *½ tsp dry yeast*
- *½ cup grated Parmesan cheese*
- *4 cloves garlic, minced*
- *1 Tbsp fresh rosemary, chopped*
- *1 ½ cup warm water*

Directions
1. Combine the yeast, flour, salt, cheese, rosemary, and garlic in a large bowl.
2. Gradually pour in the water and mix well. Form a rough ball from the dough.
3. Put the dough into a large clean bowl. Cover with a kitchen towel and leave for 24 hours. After this the dough should be slightly covered in bubbles and have doubled in size.
4. Preheat the oven to 450°F and put a closed, empty Dutch oven inside for 30 minutes.
5. Transfer the dough onto a floured surface. Pull the corners of the batter underneath until a smooth ball is formed. Prepare a large piece of parchment paper and put the bread onto it. Lightly dust the batter and cover again. Leave for 15 minutes.
6. Gently pat the top of your dough with a dampened hand.
7. Take the Dutch oven out of the oven and open the lid. Put the dough into the pan by lifting corners of the paper. Cover with the lid and put back in the oven. Bake for 30 minutes.
8. Remove the lid and bake uncovered for 10 minutes.
9. Take out of the oven and let it cool on a rack for 30 – 40 minutes before serving.

Vegan Artisan Bread

SERVINGS: **1** PREP TIME: **1 h. 30 min.** COOK TIME: **30 min.**

CARBS – **38 g** FAT – **1 g** PROTEIN – **5 g** CALORIES – **185**

Ingredients

- *3½ – 4 cups all – purpose flour*
- *1 package instant yeast*
- *1 tsp salt*
- *1½ cups dairy – free milk*
- *¼ cup maple syrup*

Directions

1. Mix the yeast, flour, and salt in a large bowl. Pour in the milk and then the maple syrup.
2. Fold to combine well using a wooden spatula. Dust the dough with flour if it is sticky and make a ball.
3. Grease the bowl and put the dough into it. Cover using a kitchen towel and leave for 1 hour 30 minutes in a warm place to double in size.
4. 30 minutes before the dough has risen, preheat oven to 450°F and put a closed and empty Dutch oven inside.
5. Flour the work surface and transfer the bread onto it. Lightly dust the top of the dough and pull all of its sides onto the top.
6. Prepare some parchment paper and put the bread on it seam side up.
7. Take out the preheated Dutch oven and remove the lid. Lift up your bread by holding the corners of the paper and lower it into the Dutch oven. Close and bake for 30 minutes.
8. Then remove the lid and bake uncovered for 10 – 15 minutes until the top has a nice brown crust.
9. Take out the bread and put onto a cooling rack and let it cool for 30 – 45 minutes before slicing and serving.

No – Knead Whole – Wheat Bread

SERVINGS: 1 PREP TIME: 10 min. + 12 – 18 h. COOK TIME: 45 min.

CARBS – 21 g FAT – 1 g PROTEIN – 4 g CALORIES – 90

Ingredients
- *2 ¼ cups bread flour, + more for the work surface*
- *¾ cup whole – wheat flour*
- *1 ¼ tsp table salt*
- *½ tsp active dry yeast*
- *1 ⅓ cups cool water (55 – 65°F)*
- *Additional flour for dusting*

Directions
1. Mix the flours, salt, and yeast in a large bowl. Pour in the water and mix for 30 seconds – 1 minute to get sticky and wet dough.
2. Cover it using a kitchen towel and let it sit for 12 – 18 hours at room temperature to double in size.
3. Scrape the dough onto a floured work surface. Lift the edges to the center of the dough using your hands. Nudge and tuck in the edges to round them.
4. Dust a clean kitchen towel well. Put the dough onto it (seam side down). If it feels sticky, lightly dust the top with flour.
5. Cover the bread with another towel and leave in a warm place for 1 – 2 hours to double in size. It's ready when it's doubled in size, and the dough holds the impression if you poke it. If it doesn't, leave for 15 more minutes.
6. Preheat the oven to 475°F and put the closed and empty Dutch oven into it for 30 minutes.
7. When the dough is ready take out the Dutch oven and carefully transfer the bread onto it seam side up. Close the lid and bake for 30 minutes. Then remove the lid and bake uncovered for 15 – 30 minutes to the desired crust.
8. Take the bread out of the oven and let it cool for 30 minutes on a cooling rack before slicing.

Harvest Grain Bread

SERVINGS: **1** PREP TIME: **15 min. + 9 hours** COOK TIME: **50 min.**

CARBS – **30 g** FAT – **1 g** PROTEIN – **6 g** CALORIES – **153**

Ingredients

- *3¼ cups high – gluten flour*
- *1 cup whole wheat flour*
- *1 cup harvest grains blend*
- *2 tsp salt*
- *1 tsp instant yeast*
- *1¾ cups cool water*

Directions

1. Mix all of the dry ingredients in a bowl, then pour in the water. Mix with your hands until it's a sticky dough and the flour has been incorporated. Knead for 2 – 3 minutes to make it smooth.
2. Cover it using a kitchen towel and let it rest overnight (8 hours at room temperature). It should rise a bit and become bubbly.
3. Place the dough onto a floured surface and form a round loaf.
4. Grease a crock and place the dough into it, smooth side up. Cover with a lid and leave for 1 hour 30 minutes. It will help to settle and expand the dough.
5. Next, slash the top of the bread with pattern to allow expansion and transfer the crock with the bread into a cold oven and set to 450°F.
6. Bake for 45 – 50 minutes. Remove the lid and bake uncovered for 5 – 15 more minutes to get a beautiful brown crust.
7. Take out of the oven and let the bread cool on a rack for 30 – 45 minutes before slicing.

No – Knead Brioche Bread

SERVINGS: 1 PREP TIME: 40 min. + overnight COOK TIME: 30 min.

CARBS – 15 g FAT – 6 g PROTEIN – 4 g CALORIES – 130

Ingredients
- *2 cups all – purpose flour*
- *7 Tbsp dairy butter, melted*
- *⅓ cup milk at room temperature*
- *2 eggs*
- *2½ Tbsp honey*
- *1 tsp salt*
- *1 tsp instant dried yeast*

Directions
1. Mix the salt, flour, and yeast in a large mixing bowl.
2. In another bowl, whisk the eggs, honey, milk, salt, and butter together.
3. Add this mixture to the dry ingredients and mix for 30 seconds to get a smooth dough without lumps. Cover it and leave for 2 hours at room temperature.
4. Then knock the air out of the dough using a spatula. Cover it and then put it in the fridge overnight.
5. When ready to bake, remove the dough from the fridge and warm to room temperature.
6. Transfer your dough onto a floured work surface and shape it into the form you want.
7. Cover with cling wrap and leave for 2 – 3 hours to double in size.
8. Preheat the oven to 375ºF and brush your soft brioche with beaten egg wash before putting in the oven.
9. Bake for 25 – 30 minutes until the bread is a golden brown color all over.
10. Take it out of the oven and let it cool completely before slicing.

Oregano Garlic Bread

SERVINGS: 1 PREP TIME: 25 min. + 3h. COOK TIME: 45 min.

CARBS – 32 g FAT – 7 g PROTEIN – 5 g CALORIES – 221

Ingredients

- *1½ tsp active dry yeast*
- *1 cup warm water, 110 – 115°F*
- *2 tsp white sugar*
- *2 tsp fine salt*
- *3 Tbsp extra virgin olive oil + extra to brush*
- *Coarse sea salt for sprinkling on top*
- *2½ cups bread flour*
- *1 Tbsp dried rosemary*
- *¼ tsp freshly ground black pepper*
- *½ tsp dried oregano*
- *1 head of roasted garlic*

Directions

1. Add the yeast to warm water. Add in the sugar and salt. Leave until it starts to foam. Add in the oil and flour and knead for 10 minutes.
2. Add the oregano, pepper, and rosemary. Knead for 5 more minutes. Next, carefully knead in the garlic with your hands for 1 minute. While kneading the dough form a ball.
3. Transfer the dough ball into an oiled bowl and turn it to coat with oil from all sides. Tightly cover using plastic wrap and leave for 1 – 2 hours to double in size.
4. Then punch the dough down and form a rounded loaf. Make a crisscross cut on top with a sharp knife.
5. Place the dough onto the baking sheet seam side up. Cover it up with a large bowl and leave for 1 hour to rise again.
6. Then brush the dough with olive oil and sprinkle with rosemary and salt. Put into the oven and bake for 25 – 30 minutes at 375°F. You need to spray it with water once in the middle of baking.
7. Set the oven to 425°F and spray the bread with water again. Bake until you get a beautiful golden – brown crust.
8. Take out and put on a cooling rack and let it cool for 40 minutes before slicing.

Multigrain Bread

SERVINGS: 1 PREP TIME: 3 h. 40 min. COOK TIME: 45 min.

CARBS – 22 g FAT – 2 g PROTEIN – 7 g CALORIES – 138

Ingredients
- ¼ cup rolled oats
- ¼ cup quinoa
- ¼ cup sunflower seeds
- ¼ cup water
- 3 cups lukewarm water
- 1 Tbsp active yeast
- 1½ Tbsp kosher salt
- 4 cups all – purpose flour
- 1 cup whole wheat flour
- 1 cup rye flour

Directions
1. Combine the quinoa, oats, sunflower seeds, and water in a bowl. Leave for 1 hour.
2. Mix the water and yeast in a large bowl. Mix in the kosher salt, flours, soaked oats, and seeds using a wooden spoon. Mix to combine. You don't need to knead the dough.
3. Cover using a kitchen towel and leave for 2 hours to double in size.
4. Flour the surface and evenly divide the batter into two balls. Dust them if needed, and stretch the edges of the dough underneath to shape it into two loaves.
5. Dust some parchment paper with cornmeal. Transfer the loaves onto the paper. Let them rest for 40 minutes.
6. Preheat the oven to 450ºF. Put your pizza stone on the center rack. Also, put a pan on the bottom rack (for steaming).

7. Next, lightly flour both dough balls and make few cuts along with the bread with a sharp knife.

8. Slide the loaves onto the pizza stone as far apart as possible. Carefully pour 1 cup of hot water into the pan and close the oven to fill it with steam.

9. Bake for 35 minutes to get a crispy and brown crust. Take it out and let the loaves cool on a rack for 30 minutes before slicing.

Asiago Bread

SERVINGS: 1 PREP TIME: 3 h. 30 min. COOK TIME: 45 min.

CARBS – 23 g FAT – 3 g PROTEIN – 4 g CALORIES – 134

Ingredients

- *3½ to 3¾ cups bread flour*
- *1 tsp sugar*
- *2¼ tsp fast – acting dry yeast*
- *1¼ cups warm water 120°F – 130°F*
- *2 Tbsp olive or vegetable oil*
- *2 tsp dried rosemary or thyme leaves*
- *1 tsp salt*
- *1¼ cup diced Asiago cheese*

Directions

1.   Add 1½ cups flour, sugar, and yeast to a large bowl and mix. Pour in the warm water. Whisk with an electric mixer for 1 minute at a low speed while scraping the bowl a few times. Cover with a towel and leave for 1 hour.
2.   Add in the rosemary, oil, and salt and stir. While stirring, gradually add ½ cup of flour at a time to form a smooth, soft dough. Let it stand for 15 minutes.
3.   Put the dough on a lightly floured surface. Knead until your dough is springy and smooth. Add 1 cup of cheese and knead again.
4.   Oil a large bowl and transfer your dough into it, turning it to coat each side. Using plastic wrap, cover it tightly, and leave for 1 hour to double in size.
5.   Grease a baking paper piece and place the batter on the floured surface. Shape the bread into a 12" long loaf – stretch its sides downward to create a smooth top.
6.   Transfer the loaf onto a sheet smooth side up. Dust it with flour thoroughly and cover using plastic wrap. Leave for 1 hour to rise.
7.   Put a pan on the bottom rack of the oven. Pour hot water into the pan (½" from top). Heat oven to 450°F.

8.   Lightly dampen the bread with cool water and sprinkle with flour. Make a ½" –
deep slash lengthwise down center of bread (use a serrated knife). Sprinkle the
slash with ¼ cup of cheese.
9.   Bake for 10 minutes, then reduce to 400°F. Bake for 20 – 25 more minutes to
make it a deep golden color.
10. Take it out from the oven and let it cool for 40 minutes before slicing.

Rosemary Garlic Bread

SERVINGS: 1 PREP TIME: 5 min. + 18 h. COOK TIME: 45 min.

CARBS – 29 g FAT – 1 g PROTEIN – 4 g CALORIES – 155

Ingredients

- *1 head garlic, roasted*
- *1 Tbsp olive oil*
- *3 cups all – purpose flour*
- *1½ tsp kosher salt*
- *½ tsp active dry yeast*
- *1½ cups room temperature water*
- *1 Tbsp fresh rosemary, chopped*

Directions

1.   Add the flour, yeast, salt, rosemary, and roasted garlic to a large bowl. Pour in the water and mix to combine until you start to get a very shaggy dough.
2.   Next, cover with plastic wrap and leave for 12 – 18 hours in a warm place.
3.   When it's ready to bake, put a closed and empty a Dutch oven into the oven and preheat it to 450°F.
4.   Put your dough onto a floured spice and form a ball using floured hands. It should be very sticky.
5.   Transfer the loaf to a piece of parchment paper and take out the preheated Dutch oven.
6.   Note, you can feel free not to use the parchment paper for this recipe. Slash the bread on top with a pattern to allow expansion.
7.   Put your bread into the Dutch oven, close the lid, and bake for 30 minutes. Then, remove the lid and bake uncovered for 10 – 15 minutes to get a beautiful golden – brown crust.
8.   Take out of the oven and transfer your bread to a cooling rack. Let it cool for 30 – 45 minutes before slicing.

Artisan Rolls

SERVINGS: **1** PREP TIME: **20 min. + 12 h.** COOK TIME: **40 min.**

CARBS – **22 g** FAT – **1 g** PROTEIN – **4 g** CALORIES – **115**

Ingredients
- *4 cups bread flour + extra for shaping*
- *2 tsp kosher salt*
- *1 tsp active dry yeast*
- *2 cups room temperature tap water*

Directions
1.   Mix the salt, flour, and yeast in a large bowl. Then, make a well in the center of the mixture and pour in the water. Using a rubber spatula, mix until flour is incorporated to get a wet and sticky dough.
2.   Cover using plastic wrap and leave for 12 hours in a warm place to rise. The dough should rise, become shaggy, and be covered in bubbles.
3.   Prepare a sheet pan: line it with a piece of parchment paper. Preheat the oven to 425ºF.
4.   Flour the work surface well. Put your dough onto it and turn to coat with flour.
5.   Divide your dough evenly into 12 – 16 portions, and turn all the pieces in the flour to coat. Then, form into balls by pulling the edges underneath and pinch them together to make a smooth top. Invert them and transfer to the pan pinched side up to get rustic textured rolls. Leave them for 20 minutes to rise. Slash the bread top with a pattern to allow expansion.
6.   Put the pan into the oven and bake for 15 minutes. After 15 minutes, rotate the pan and bake for an additional 5 minutes.
7.   Take out the rolls from the oven and put them on a cooling rack. Let them cool completely.

No – Knead Sandwich Bread

SERVINGS: 2 PREP TIME: 10 min. + 7 h. COOK TIME: 40 min.

CARBS – 18 g FAT – 1 g PROTEIN – 3 g CALORIES – 93

Ingredients
- 3¼ cups bread flour
- 3¼ cups all – purpose flour
- 2 tsp instant or active dry yeast
- 1½ Tbsp kosher salt
- 3 cups water

Directions
1.   Add and mix the yeast, flours, and salt in a large bowl. Pour in the water and mix to get a shaggy dough using a wooden spatula. Cover using a tea towel and leave for 5 hours.
2.   When it's done, put the dough onto a floured work surface. Knead it 4 – 5 times. Divide it evenly into two portions. Only bake one loaf and save the second one for the future. Form a rectangle (8"x12") from one portion.
3.   Then, fold one – third of your dough to the center, do the same with another third. Transfer the dough into a greased loaf pan seam side down. Cover and leave for 1 hour to rise.
4.   Preheat the oven to 450°F. Lightly sprinkle the top of the bread with flour. Bake for 35 minutes or more to get a nice brown top.
5.   Take out of the oven and transfer to a cooling rack. Let it cool for 40 minutes before slicing.

Jalapeno Cheese Bread

SERVINGS: 1 PREP TIME: 2 h. 10 min. COOK TIME: 50 min.

CARBS – 40 g FAT – 13 g PROTEIN – 14 g CALORIES – 339

Ingredients

- *3½ cups bread flour plus more for dusting*
- *2½ cups shredded cheddar cheese, divided*
- *1 jalapeño, seeded and coarsely chopped*
- *1 jalapeño, sliced into rings, divided*
- *1 Tbsp kosher salt*
- *2 cups warm water*
- *2¼ tsp instant yeast*
- *1 Tbsp olive oil*

Directions

1. Mix the bread flour, 2 cups of cheese, chopped jalapeños, and salt in a large bowl. Stir well.
2. In another large bowl, combine the yeast and warm water. Pour the flour mixture over the water and stir with a silicone spatula until it comes together as a dough.
3. Fold your dough around the edges of the bowl to the center with a spatula, while you rotate the bowl each time. Fold 8 – 9 times. Cover with a towel and leave for 60 minutes in a warm place. When it's done, repeat the same process and leave again for 30 minutes, covered with a towel.
4. Preheat the oven to 450°F and put a closed Dutch oven into it for 30 minutes.
5. Flour your hands and a work surface. Transfer the dough onto it, then flip over and remove all the excess flour with a brush. Fold the edges of the dough to the center 8 times. Flip it over and put on a piece of parchment paper.
6. Oil the top of the bread with a brush, sprinkle it with the rest of the cheese and the jalapeno rings. Slash the bread top with a pattern to allow expansion.
7. Put your bread in a preheated Dutch oven by lifting up the corners of the paper. Close it with the lid on and bake for 30 minutes, then remove the lid and bake uncovered for a further 20 minutes.
8. Take out of the oven and let it cool for 1 hour before slicing.

SOURDOUGH BREAD
Sourdough Starter

SERVINGS: **1** PREP TIME: **1 week** COOK TIME: **5 min.**

CARBS – **95 g** FAT – **1 g** PROTEIN – **13 g** CALORIES – **455**

Ingredients
- *1 cup all – purpose flour*
- *½ cup water*

Directions
1.   Add the flour and water to a large glass container and stir together. Loosely cover with plastic wrap. Leave in a warm place for 1 day.
2.   Pour in an additional ½ cup of water and add 1 cup of flour. Cover loosely and leave in a warm place for 1 day again. Feed your starter every day for 1 week or until it looks very bubbly and aromatic. The starter is ready for baking now.
3.   If not using it, keep the starter in the fridge and feed once a week. When you're ready to use it, let the starter warm to room temperature before cooking and remove the needed amount. Continue to feed the remaining starter and leave for 1 day at room temperature before chilling.
4.   If you have too much starter in the container, remove half before feeding it and discard it.

Gluten – Free Sourdough Starter

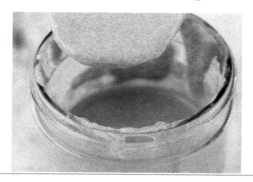

SERVINGS: 1 PREP TIME: 1 day COOK TIME: 5 min.

CARBS – 23 g FAT – 1 g PROTEIN – 2 g CALORIES – 120

Ingredients
- *50 g brown teff flour gluten – free*
- *100 g water*

Directions
1. Mix the teff flour and water with clean hands in a grease – free bowl.
2. Pour the mixture into a grease – free glass jar and cover it with a non – airtight lid.
3. Leave the jar for 18 – 24 hours at room temperature.
4. If you are not planning to use it, keep it in the fridge (it will slow down the process of fermentation), keep feeding it every two days with fresh water and flour.

Classic Sourdough Bread

SERVINGS: 2 PREP TIME: 20 min. + 8 h. COOK TIME: 25 min.

CARBS – 21 g FAT – 1 g PROTEIN – 3 g CALORIES – 103

Ingredients

- *In 3½ – 3¾ cups all – purpose flour*
- *1½ cups warm water 105°F – 115°F*
- *1 cup sourdough starter, room temperature*
- *1 Tbsp salt*

Directions

1.   Add 3 cups of flour, the starter, and water in a large bowl and mix until smooth. Cover with plastic wrap and leave in a warm place for 4 hours. Then, put it into the fridge and let it chill overnight.

2.   Stir in the remaining flour and salt. Then, transfer the dough onto a floured surface. Knead it more to get a smooth dough, adding extra flour if needed. Put into an oiled bowl and turn it to coat with oil. Cover with plastic wrap and leave for 2 hours at room temperature. It should increase in size a little and be slightly covered with a few bubbles.

3.   Use parchment paper to line a large baking sheet. Put the dough onto a floured work surface. Carefully divide the dough in half. Shape each portion into an oval loaf. Transfer both loaves onto a lined baking sheet, then cover with greased plastic wrap. Leave for 2 hours to double in size.

4.   Preheat the oven to 425°F. Make three diagonal cuts cross the tops of the loaves using a sharp knife. Put into the oven and bake for 25 – 30 minutes to get golden crust.

5.   Remove from the oven and let it fully cool before serving on a cooling rack.

Artisan Sourdough Bread

SERVINGS: **1** PREP TIME: **20 min. + 12 h.** COOK TIME: **45 min.**

CARBS – **32 g** FAT – **2 g** PROTEIN – **6 g** CALORIES – **162**

Ingredients
- *1 cup active sourdough starter (100% hydration)*
- *1 cup warm water*
- *2½ cups unbleached all – purpose flour*
- *1½ tsp table salt*
- *Rice flour for proofing basket*

Directions
1. Mix the water, starter, and 1½ cups flour in a stand mixer bowl. Fit the paddle and mix at a low speed to get a thick batter. Then, cover with a kitchen towel and leave for 30 – 60 minutes in a warm place.
2. Fit the dough hook and add the remaining flour and salt. Mix until it starts to form a ball. The dough should be quite sticky.
3. Transfer the dough into another greased bowl and turn it to coat with oil. Cover and leave for 30 minutes at room temperature.
4. Then, lift one dough side and fold into the middle. Repeat with the other three sides, then flip your dough over. Cover the bowl again and leave for 30 minutes. Repeat this process and then leave for 1 hour. After an hour, repeat again. The dough might be airy, elastic, and lively. If it's sluggish, leave it for 1 – 2 hours at room temperature. Cover tightly, using plastic wrap, and put in the fridge overnight.
5. Next, dump the dough onto the floured work surface. Form a smooth ball with your hands without kneading. Cover loosely with plastic wrap and leave for 20 – 30 minutes to rest.
6. Uncover and knead twice. Shape it into a smooth ball and transfer it onto the lined baking sheet.

7.   Cover and leave for 1 – 2 hours at room temperature until the dough has doubled in size. When you poke it, it should spring back. Slash the bread on the top with a pattern to allow expansion.

8.   Preheat the oven to 425°F. Put an empty and closed Dutch oven inside.

9.   Take out the preheated pan and open the lid. Lift the dough up by holding parchment paper and lower into the Dutch oven.

10. Close the lid and put into the oven. Bake for 20 minutes, then remove the lid and bake for 20 more minutes to get a nice brown crust on top of the loaf.

11. Take it out of the Dutch oven and transfer the bread onto the oven rack by holding the parchment paper. Bake for an additional 5 – 10 minutes.

12. When it's ready, take your bread out of the oven and let it cool for 40 minutes before slicing.

No – Knead Sourdough Bread

SERVINGS: 1 PREP TIME: 30 min. + 10 h. COOK TIME: 1 h.

CARBS – 34 g FAT – 6 g PROTEIN – 8 g CALORIES – 158

Ingredients

- 4 cups +2 Tbsp bread flour
- ¼ cup bubbly, active starter
- 1½ tsp fine sea salt
- 1⅓ cups + 2 Tbsp warm water

Directions

1.   Whisk the water and starter in a large bowl using a fork. Add the salt and flour. Mix to get a stiff dough, then mix with your hands to make sure that the flour has been totally incorporated. The dough should be shaggy, dense, and sticky to touch. Use a damp towel to cover the bowl and leave for 30 minutes.

2.   Then form a smooth bowl from the dough – grab one dough side and fold it over by pressing it into the center with your fingertips. Repeat until it starts to become tight.

3.   Cover with towel again and leave for 8 – 10 hours at room temperature to double in size.

4.   Place the dough onto the floured surface. Shape it into a round shape by folding the top of the dough over and to the center. Turn the dough a little and fold over another part of the dough. Repeat this process to get a full dough circle. Flip it over and leave for 5 – 10 minutes.

5.   Meanwhile, line an 8" bowl with a dusted towel. Flour your hands and cup the dough in to you with a circular motion. Transfer the dough into the bowl seam side up.

6.   Cover, then leave it for 30 minutes – 1 hour. The dough is ready to bake when it's puffy and slightly risen.

7.   Preheat the oven to 450°F and prepare a large piece of parchment paper. Place the piece of paper over your dough and invert the bowl to release. Sprinkle the

bread with flour and rub its surface with your hands. Make one cut on the top with a sharp knife. Place the dough into the baking pot using the parchment paper.

8.   Bake with the lid closed for 20 minutes on the middle rack. Remove the lid and bake for 30 more minutes. Then, take the bread out of the pot and place it on the oven rack. Bake for an additional 10 minutes to get a beautiful brown crust.

9.   Take out of the oven and let it cool completely on a cooling rack before slicing.

Multigrain Sourdough Bread

SERVINGS: **1** PREP TIME: **20 min. + overnight** COOK TIME: **30 min.**

CARBS – **31 g** FAT – **2 g** PROTEIN – **5 g** CALORIES – **168**

Ingredients

For the soaker:
- ¾ cup boiling water
- ¾ cup harvest grains mix
- 1 tsp salt

For the dough:
- All of the soaker
- ¾ cup fed sourdough starter
- ½ cup warm water
- 1½ cups whole wheat flour
- 1½ cups unbleached bread flour
- 1 tsp salt
- 1½ tsp active dry yeast
- 2 Tbsp vegetable oil

Directions

1.   Mix the boiling water, salt, and grains mixture in a bowl. Cover lightly using plastic wrap and leave overnight in a warm place.
2.   Then, combine the soaker with the rest of the dough ingredients. Mix it with your hands to get a soft dough.
3.   Transfer the dough into a greased bowl, cover and leave for 1 – 1 hour 30 minutes until almost double the size.
4.   Then, fold it over 3 – 4 times on a greased work surface. Form an 11" log, and transfer it onto a baking sheet lined with parchment paper. Cover your bread and leave for 1 – 1 hour 30 minutes.
5.   Preheat the oven to 425°F.
6.   Slash the bread top with a pattern to allow expansion.
7.   Bake for 20 minutes. Set to 350°F, and bake for 10 – 15 more minutes until you get a golden – brown bread.
8.   Remove and transfer onto a rack to cool completely before serving.

Rosemary Olive Sourdough Bread

SERVINGS: 2 PREP TIME: 20 min. + 3 h. COOK TIME: 30 min.

CARBS – 25 g FAT – 1 g PROTEIN – 4 g CALORIES – 130

Ingredients
- *1 cup sourdough starter, ripe*
- *1¼ cups lukewarm water*
- *¼ cup olive oil*
- *2 tsp instant yeast*
- *1 Tbsp sugar*
- *2½ tsp salt*
- *2 cloves garlic, finely chopped*
- *1 Tbsp fresh oregano, finely chopped*
- *4½ – 4¾ cups unbleached all – purpose flour*
- *½ – 1 cup kalamata olives, coarsely chopped*

Directions
1. Add all of the ingredients (except the olives) to a large bowl, then mix and knead to create a smooth dough. Fold in the olives.
2. Cover using plastic wrap and leave for 1 hour 30 minutes to double in size.
3. Then divide your dough in half.
4. Form a round loaf from each portion. Put the loaves onto a lightly greased baking sheet.
5. Cover and leave for 1 hour to allow to rise. It should become very puffy. Preheat the oven to 425°F.
6. Dampen your bread with lukewarm water, and, using sharp knife, make two deep diagonal slashes on the tops.
7. Bake for 25 – 30 minutes until they have a deep golden – brown color.
8. Take out of the oven and let them cool completely before slicing.

Gluten – Free Sourdough Bread

SERVINGS: **1** PREP TIME: **3 h.** COOK TIME: **1 h. 30 min.**

CARBS – **23 g** FAT – **1 g** PROTEIN – **2 g** CALORIES – **120**

Ingredients

- *3 cups gluten – free all – purpose flour*
- *¼ cup cassava flour*
- *¼ cup dry milk powder*
- *½ tsp baking soda*
- *2 tsp baking powder*
- *1 tsp sea salt*
- *¾ cup gluten – free sourdough starter*
- *1¼ cups naturally gluten – free beer*
- *2 large eggs*
- *2 Tbsp apple cider vinegar*
- *¼ cup olive oil*
- *¼ cup sugar*
- *1 Tbsp psyllium husk powder*

Directions

1.   Preheat the oven to 200°F.
2.   Beat the eggs, oil, vinegar, psyllium husk powder, sugar and starter. Mix for 2 – 4 minutes until it becomes smooth and thick. Gradually stir the dry components into the bubbly liquid using a wooden spoon until the dough is smooth, and all dry ingredients have been fully incorporated.
3.   Put the dough into oiled Pullman Pan, dusted with a bit of gluten – free flour. Dust the dough top with more gluten – free flour and lightly brush with olive oil. Cover with oiled plastic wrap and put into the oven. Turn off the heat and turn the light on.
4.   Let it rest for 1 hour 30 minutes – 3 hours before baking the bread. Take out of the oven.
5.   Preheat the oven to 325°F with convection.
6.   Remove the wrap and make a few slashes on the top of the bread as pictured.
7.   Bake for 1 hour 15 minutes.
8.   Take out of the oven and let it cool in the pan for 15 minutes. Then, remove from the pan and cool completely before slicing.

French Sourdough Bread

SERVINGS: 2 – 3 PREP TIME: 2 h. COOK TIME: 50 min.

CARBS – 22 g FAT – 1 g PROTEIN – 4 g CALORIES – 120

Ingredients

- *2¾ cups warm water 93°F*
- *5¾ cups strong white flour*
- *½ cup wheat or rye whole grain flour*
- *1 Tbsp amaranth*
- *1⅓ cups sourdough starter*
- *1 Tbsp salt*

Directions

1.   Mix the flour and water in a bowl. Leave for 15 – 30 minutes to hydrate the flour. Then, stir in the starter and salt.
2.   Let it rise for 6 – 12 hours in a warm place loosely covered with plastic wrap until it's doubled in size. Wet your hands to avoid sticking. Grab a handful of the dough and carefully pull to the side and fold over the top. Fold the dough 2 – 3 more times, then let it rest for 30 minutes before repeating this folding process 3 – 4 more times during the 6 – 12 hours of resting.
3.   Transfer the dough onto a floured surface, divide evenly into 2 pieces by cutting the dough.
4.   Gently from two balls from the dough, avoid kneading it and use as much flour as you need.
5.   Prepare two large bowls and line them with well – floured tea towels. Transfer your dough balls into the bowls and leave for 2 hours to rest or refrigerate overnight with an air – tight lid.
6.   Preheat the oven to 500°F. Put a closed Dutch oven inside to preheat it.
7.   Gently put the loaf on a large piece of parchment paper and lift it into the preheated Dutch oven. Slash the bread top with a pattern to allow expansion.
8.   Bake covered for 30 minutes. Then uncover the Dutch oven and bake for 20 more minutes until it turns nice dark brown color.
9.   Take out of the oven and let your bread cool completely before slicing.

Sage and Caramelized Onion Bread

SERVINGS: 1 PREP TIME: 20 min. + 3 hours COOK TIME: 55 min.

CARBS – 58 g FAT – 2 g PROTEIN – 8 g CALORIES – 286

Ingredients

For the sponge:
- 22 g sourdough starter
- ¾ cup all – purpose flour plain flour
- ½ cup water lukewarm

For caramelized onions:
- ½ onion, finely diced
- ½ Tbsp olive oil + extra
- ¼ tsp sugar
- ¼ tsp salt
- ½ tsp fresh sage, finely diced

For the loaf:
- 1¾ cups all – purpose flour (plain flour)
- 1 cup whole – wheat flour
- ¾ cup water lukewarm
- ½ Tbsp salt
- 1 lime, sliced into wedges

Directions

1. Combine the sponge ingredients in a bowl and mix well. Cover with a cling wrap and leave overnight at room temperature. You will see that bubbles have formed on top.

2. Caramelize the onion: heat the oil in a small skillet over a medium heat. Add the onion, salt, and sugar. Cook for 15 – 20 minutes until the onion is soft. Lower the temperature and add more oil to avoid burning. When the onion starts to caramelize, add the sage and cook for 2 – 3 minutes. Turn it off and allow to cool.

3. When the sponge has risen, add additional water and flour without salt. Leave for 30 minutes to rest.
4. Then, add the salt and mix. Turn your sponge onto a floured work surface. Spread the mixture out slightly and top with the onion. Fold in the sides, then knead for 2 minutes – push one side out with the heel of your hand, fold over, turn 90°and repeat. Form a ball.
5. Oil a bowl and put the ball inside. Cover and leave for 2 hours, repeating the folding process every 30 minutes by pulling on one side, stretching it up as far as it goes, and folding it over the dough. Turn the bowl 90° and repeat 4 – 6 times. Meanwhile, line a Dutch oven with parchment paper.
6. Next, place your dough onto the floured work surface. From a tight ball by folding each side over into the middle. Repeat again with floured hands and shape into a ball. Transfer the dough into the Dutch oven smooth side up.
7. Cover with cling wrap and leave for 2 hours.
8. Then, take the dough out of the Dutch oven by holding the parchment paper. Preheat the oven to 450°F with the closed Dutch oven inside.
9. Take out the Dutch oven and carefully lower your loaf into it by holding the parchment paper. Bake covered for 30 minutes, then uncover the bread and bake for 20 minutes to get a golden – brown loaf.
10. Take out of the oven and let it completely cool on a cooling rack before slicing.

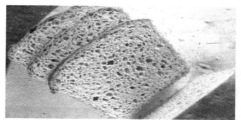

Whole – Wheat Sourdough Bread

SERVINGS: 2 PREP TIME: 20 min. + 2 h. COOK TIME: 40 min.

CARBS – 21 g FAT – 2 g PROTEIN – 4 g CALORIES – 114

Ingredients

- *2 cups sourdough starter*
- *2 cups water*
- *4 – 5 cups whole wheat flour*
- *1 Tbsp sugar or molasses*
- *2 tsp salt*
- *1 Tbsp cornmeal*
- *2 tsp apple cider vinegar*

Directions

1.   Add the starter, water, 2 cups of flour, and sugar. Mix well and leave for 9 hours or overnight.
2.   Beat the dough in a stand mixer fitted with the kneading attachment. Add the vinegar, salt, and 1 cup of flour. Continue to mix the dough and add the flour (¼ cup at a time) to get a slightly sticky dough that doesn't stick to the sides.
3.   Knead in the mixer for 5 minutes. You should get a smooth, supple, and not too firm dough ball. If it isn't, gradually add flour, 1 tsp at time.
4.   Oil a bowl and put the ball inside, turn to coat the top with oil.
5.   Cover the bowl with cling wrap leave for 2 hours in a warm place to double in size.
6.   Grease two loaf pans with oil, sprinkle the sides and bottom of the pans with cornmeal.
7.   Punch the dough down and divide into two portions. Shape each piece into a loaf – roll it out into a 6" wide and 9" long rectangle then roll it into a log. Then, tuck all of the sides down and pinch the seams. Transfer the loaves into greased loaf pans seam side down. Cover with shower caps and leave for 2 hours in a warm place.
8.   Preheat the oven to 425°F.
9.   Bake the loaves for 40 minutes on the central oven rack. Take out of the oven and let them cool completely before slicing.

Cinnamon Raisin Sourdough Bread

SERVINGS: 1 PREP TIME: 2 h. 25 min. COOK TIME: 45 min.

CARBS – 37 g FAT – 4 g PROTEIN – 4 g CALORIES – 194

Ingredients
- ½ cup sourdough starter, ripe
- 3 cups unbleached all – purpose flour
- 2 ½ tsp instant yeast
- 1 Tbsp sugar
- 1 ¼ tsp salt
- 1 large egg
- 5 Tbsp butter, softened
- ⅔ cup lukewarm water

For the filling:
- ¼ cup sugar
- 1 ½ tsp cinnamon
- 1 large egg + 1 Tbsp water, beaten
- 2 tsp unbleached all – purpose flour
- ½ cup raisins

Directions
1.   Mix all of the dough ingredients in a bowl and knead it with your hands to form a soft, smooth dough. Transfer the dough into a greased container and leave for 1 hour 30 minutes – 2 hours to double in size.
2.   Mix the cinnamon, sugar, and flour in a bowl to make the filling.
3.   Then, deflate your dough and place onto a greased work surface. Roll and pat the dough into a 6" x 20" rectangle.
4.   Brush it with the egg and water mixture and spread it evenly with the filling and raisins, leaving a 1" wide border off one of the short edges.

5. Beginning with another short end that's covered with filling, roll your dough into a log. Seal the ends by pinching them, also pinch the long seam closed.

6. Place the log into greased 9" x 5" loaf pan seam – side down. Cover and leave for 1 hour until it's crested a little over the pan rim.

7. Preheat the oven to 350°F and bake for 15 – 20 minutes tented with foil, then remove the foil and bake for 30 – 35 minutes more. It should have a golden – brown crust.

8. Remove from the oven and transfer onto a cooling rack. Brush the top with butter while hot, then let it cool completely before slicing.

Vegan Whole – Wheat Sourdough Bread

SERVINGS: 2 PREP TIME: 15 min. + 18 h. COOK TIME: 35 min.

CARBS – 49 g FAT – 1 g PROTEIN – 7 g CALORIES – 230

Ingredients

- *6 cups unbleached all – purpose flour, divided*
- *2¼ tsp active dry yeast*
- *3¾ cups + ⅓ cup pure water, warm 110° – 115°F, divided*
- *2 Tbsp agave syrup*
- *2 cups whole – wheat flour*
- *1 Tbsp cornmeal, for dusting*
- *2 tsp salt*

Directions

1.   Mix the yeast and 2 cups of flour in the sterile 2 – quart glass. Slowly stir in 2 cups of water to create a pasty, thick mixture. Cover using a kitchen towel and leave for 3 – 4 days at room temperature, stirring once a day. It should become bubbly and have pleasant sour smell. If you see an orange or pink tint and it smells bad, throw it away and start again.
2.   Refresh 1 cup of starter by mixing it with 1 cup of unbleached all – purpose flour and ¾ cup of water in a large bowl. Mix until well – combined and leave for 4 hours to sit.
3.   Stir in 1⅓ cups of water and syrup. In another bowl whisk the rest of the all – purpose flour, whole – wheat flour, and salt. Slowly add the flour mixture into the sourdough starter, adding a small portion of extra water if needed. Mix until the flour has been fully incorporated. The dough should be stiff. Cover and leave for 6 – 8 hours to rise.
4.   Put it onto the floured surface and knead it for 5 minutes. Then, let the dough rest for 10 minutes and knead for 5 minutes more. Allow it to rest again for 10 minutes. Divide it in half and form two firm balls. Transfer them onto a nonstick baking sheet dusted with cornmeal. Cover using a towel and leave for 2 – 4 hours.
5.   Preheat the oven to 375°F. Slash the bread top with a pattern to allow expansion. Bake for 55 – 60 minutes to get a deep golden – brown crust.
6.   Take out of the oven and let the loaves cool completely before serving.

Honey Wheat Sourdough Bread

SERVINGS: 1 PREP TIME: 20 min. + 2 h. COOK TIME: 30 min.

CARBS – 16 g FAT – 1 g PROTEIN – 3 g CALORIES – 88

Ingredients

- *3¼ – 3¾ cups all – purpose flour*
- *1 cup whole wheat flour*
- *1 Tbsp active dry yeast*
- *1 cup water 110° – 115°F*
- *3 Tbsp butter, softened*
- *2 Tbsp honey*
- *2 Tbsp molasses*
- *2 cups sourdough starter*
- *3 Tbsp toasted wheat germ*
- *1 Tbsp sugar*
- *1 tsp baking soda*
- *1 tsp salt*

Directions

1.   Pour the warm water into a large bowl and dissolve the yeast. Add the honey, butter, starter, molasses, baking soda, wheat germ, 2 cups of all – purpose flour, whole wheat flour, sugar, and salt. Beat until it becomes smooth. Then, form a soft dough by stirring in the remaining all – purpose flour.
2.   Put your dough onto a floured work surface and knead for 6 – 8 minutes until it becomes an elastic and smooth dough. Put it into a greased bowl and turn to coat the top with oil. Cover and leave for 1 hour in a warm place to double in size.
3.   Next, punch your dough down. Flip it onto a floured work surface and divide it in half. Shape each piece into a loaf.
4.   Grease two 8x4" loaf pans and put your loaves inside. Cover and leave for 1 hour. They should double in size. Preheat the oven to 375°F before baking.
5.   Brush the tops with olive oil. Then, bake for 25 – 30 minutes until they turn a nice brown color.
6.   Remove from the oven and pans and transfer to a rack to cool completely before slicing.

BAGUETTES AND CIABATTAS

Sourdough Baguette

SERVINGS: 3 PREP TIME: 20 min. + 5 h. COOK TIME: 20 min.

CARBS – 14 g FAT – 00 g PROTEIN – 2 g CALORIES – 65

Ingredients
- 3¼ cups bread flour
- 1 cup sourdough starter
- 1 cup water
- 1¾ tsp fine sea salt

Directions
1. Mix the starter, flour, water, and salt. Mix with a spatula until you get a shaggy dough. Cover using a kitchen towel and leave for 30 minutes.
2. Knead for 10 minutes until the dough starts to feel smooth. Scrape the sides of the bowl and lightly oil the insides. Form a ball and put it in the bowl. Cover again and leave for 2 – 4 hours to double in size.
3. Punch the dough down on a floured surface. Make a rectangle from the dough and fold it in thirds to the middle beginning from one short side. Pinch the ends closed. Put the dough back into the bowl, cover and leave for 30 minutes. Repeat this step again.
4. Divide your dough evenly into 3 pieces.
5. Put them on a floured work surface to form baguettes. Line a rimless baking sheet with a piece of parchment paper and transfer the baguettes onto it. Cover with a kitchen towel and leave for 30 minutes.
6. Meanwhile, preheat the oven to 450°F. Put a baking sheet on the middle rack and a cast – iron skillet on the rack below. Prepare a cup of ice cubes.
7. When baguettes have almost doubled in size, cut few slashes on their tops with a knife. Lightly dampen them and place them on the hot baking sheet. Pour the ice cubes into the skillet and close the oven door. Set to 400°F and bake for 20 minutes. Bake for longer if you want your crust deep colored.
8. Take them out and let them cool for 30 minutes before slicing.

Classic French Baguette

SERVINGS: 2 PREP TIME: 20 min. + 11 h. COOK TIME: 40 min.

CARBS – 15 g FAT – 0 g PROTEIN – 3 g CALORIES – 72

Ingredients

For the poolish:
- *¾ cup bread flour*
- *6 Tbsp + 1 tsp filtered water, warm 90°F*
- *¼ tsp active dry yeast*

For the final dough:
- *1¾ cups bread flour*
- *½ cup all – purpose flour*
- *½ cup + 3 Tbsp filtered water, warm 90°F*
- *¼ tsp active dry yeast*
- *1¼ tsp kosher salt*

Directions

1. Make a poolish in advance. Mix all of the ingredients in a large bowl. Cover it with plastic wrap and leave for 8 – 10 hours.

2. Then, add all of the ingredients for the dough to the poolish. Stir well to combine. Knead it with your hands until you get a shaggy dough and leave for 30 minutes covered with plastic wrap.

3. Next, dampen your hands and pull on and stretch up one side of the dough, then fold down over the top of the dough. Repeat for each side after the rotating bowl 90 degrees when the last side is done. Cover and leave for 30 minutes. Repeat this process four times.

4. Meanwhile, prepare the equipment: set one oven rack in the middle and another at the bottom position. Put an upside down sheet pan on the middle rack. Preheat the oven to 500°F for 1 hour. Flour a lint – free towel and line an unrimmed baking sheet with parchment paper.

5.   Divide the dough in two equal portions by cutting it. Place them on a lightly floured surface. Form a rectangle from one piece of dough and carefully stretch out the short ends. Fold every short end to the center, press it down with your fingertips to seal. Do the same with every long end to create a seam in the dough. Repeat this process with another piece. Cover both pieces with plastic wrap and leave for 10 minutes.

6.   Place one piece seam side up and press it into a thin rectangle. Start folding down your dough (½") and sealing it with fingerprints, beginning from the top left edge. Work across the top in the same way. Create a tight log by continuing folding down on the dough and sealing it. You should get a thin, tight log. Flip it seam side down. Roll your dough evenly into a long thin snake shape using both hands. Work it into a 14" baguette. Transfer it onto the prepared floured towel. Create the folds for holding dough's shape by pushing a towel up on both sides of the baguette. Repeat all the steps for the second portion. Cover the baguettes with plastic wrap and leave for 1 hour to rise.

7.   Carefully flip the baguettes onto parchment paper, seam side down. Cut 4 – 5 ¼" deep diagonal slashes on the top of the baguettes with a sharp knife.

8.   Prepare a small bowl filled with 2 cups of ice cubes. Open the oven and gently slide the whole piece of parchment paper with the baguettes onto the preheated sheet pan. Pour ice into the preheated skillet and close the oven door immediately. Turn the temperature down to 475°F and bake for about 25 – 40 minutes depending on what crust you want for your baguettes.

9.   Take them out of the oven and transfer to a cooling rack. Let them cool for 30 minutes before slicing.

Whole – Wheat Baguette

SERVINGS: **1** PREP TIME: **2 h 40 min.** COOK TIME: **25 min.**

CARBS – **10 g** FAT – **00 g** PROTEIN – **2 g** CALORIES – **49**

Ingredients

- *3 cups warm water, 110°F*
- *1½ Tbsp granulated yeast*
- *1½ Tbsp kosher salt*
- *2½ cups ground hard white wheat flour*
- *4 cups all – purpose flour*

Directions

1. Mix the yeast, water, and salt in a large bowl. Combine the flours in another bowl and mix well. Add the mixed flour to a bowl with water and stir with a wooden spoon. Knead with your hands if it's hard to stir. Cover with plastic wrap and leave for 4 – 5 hours until it begins to flatten on top.
2. Preheat the oven to 450°F. Place a baking stone on the central oven rack and a cast – iron skillet on a lower shelf.
3. Dust the dough top with flour and cut off a 1lb portion. Return the rested dough to the fridge.
4. Dust your dough lightly with flour and form into a ball. When it's cohesive, stretch and elongate it to create a cylinder (2" in diameter). Dust a piece of the parchment with whole wheat flour. Transfer the loaf onto the paper and leave for 20 minutes.
5. Next, lightly dampen the surface of the loaf. Make a few diagonal slashes across the top of the baguette with a serrated bread knife.
6. Transfer it onto the hot stone and pour 1 cup of hot water into the skillet. Close the oven and bake for 25 minutes or longer to get the deep brown crust.
7. Remove and let it cool for 40 minutes before slicing.

Gluten – Free French Baguette

SERVINGS: 1 PREP TIME: 10 min. + 1 h. COOK TIME: 40 min.

CARBS – 15 g FAT – 2 g PROTEIN – 2 g CALORIES – 80

Ingredients
- 1 cup gluten – free white rice flour
- ½ cup arrowroot flour
- 1½ tsp Xanthan gum
- ¾ tsp Himalayan fine salt
- ¾ cup warm water, 105 – 110°F
- 1 Tbsp pure maple syrup
- 2¼ tsp gluten – free active dry yeast
- 1 Tbsp extra virgin olive oil + some for brushing
- 2 large egg whites, at room temperature, whisked
- ½ tsp apple cider vinegar

Directions
1. Mix all of the dry ingredients in a large bowl.
2. Mix the water, maple syrup, and the yeast in another bowl. Leave it for 10 minutes until the yeast foams.
3. Add the olive oil, yeast, egg whites, and vinegar to the dry mixture. Beat for 1 minute with a mixer. Scrape the sides while mixing.
4. Put your dough onto a greased French bread pan and spoon with olive oil. Make a few slashes diagonally and brush with olive oil. Cover tightly with a kitchen towel and leave for 40 minutes in a warm place.
5. Preheat the oven to 400°F and transfer the dough into it. Bake for 35 – 40 minutes until it has a nice golden crust.
6. Take out from the oven and let it cool for 40 minutes before slicing.

Alternative French Baguettes

SERVINGS: 4 PREP TIME: 20 min. 2 h. COOK TIME: 15 min.

CARBS – 14 g FAT – 00 g PROTEIN – 3 g CALORIES – 70

Ingredients

- *Olive oil, for greasing*
- *3¾ cups strong white bread flour, plus extra for dusting*
- *2 tsp salt*
- *2 tsp fast – action yeast*
- *1½ cups 370ml/13fl oz cool water*

Directions

1.   Oil a 2¼ liter square plastic container with olive oil.
2.   Prepare a freestanding mixer with a dough hook and add salt, flour, and yeast to its bowl. Pour in the water (three – quarters) and start mixing at a slow speed. Gradually pour in the rest of the water when the dough comes together and mix for 5 – 7 minutes at a medium speed. You should get an elastic and glossy dough.
3.   Transfer the dough to the oiled container, cover and leave for 1 hour.
4.   Dust a linen baker couche and the work surface with flour. Gently place your dough onto the work surface.
5.   Divide it evenly into 4 portions. Flatten the dough and fold its sides to the center to form an oblong from each piece. Roll every piece up into a sausage with a smooth top and join through the whole length of the base. Starting from the middle, roll each piece with both hands. Make a forwards and backwards movement without heavy pressing to roll out 12" – long baguettes.
6.   Place a baguette along the edge of the couche and pleat it up against the edge of bread. Repeat for all of the baguettes – they should be lined up against each other and divided with a pleat between each. Cover with a tea towel and leave for 1 hour to double in size.
7.   Preheat the oven to 465°F and put a roasting tray in the bottom.

8.   When the dough has doubled in size, put them on the work surface and dust with flour. Make four slashes along the length of baguette with a sharp knife. Place each baguette on a baking tray.

9.   Put the bread into the oven and pour the hot water on the roasting tray for steam. Close the oven and bake for 20 – 25 minutes or longer for a deep color.

10. Take out of the oven and let the baguettes cool completely before slicing.

Seeded Pumpkin Baguette

SERVINGS: 6 PREP TIME: 20 min. + 1h. 30 min. COOK TIME: 30 min.
CARBS – 16 g FAT – 17 g PROTEIN – 7 g CALORIES – 229

Ingredients
For the bread:
- 1½ cups pumpkin puree
- 2 tsp instant yeast
- 2 Tbsp honey
- ½ cup lukewarm water
- 2 Tbsp vegetable oil

- 3½ cups all – purpose flour
- ½ cup sunflower seeds
- 2 Tbsp sesame seeds
- 1 Tbsp flax seeds
- 2 tsp salt

For the topping:
- 1 egg lightly beaten
- ¼ cup pepitas pumpkin seeds

- 1 Tbsp poppy seeds
- 2 Tbsp sunflower seeds

Directions
1.   In the stand mixer bowl (with paddle attachment) add the pumpkin puree, honey, yeast, water, oil, and 1 cup of flour. Mix well to combine at a low speed. Add the seeds and salt. Then, set the kneading hook. Slowly add in 2 cups of flour, kneading until fully incorporated. Add more flour if you still haven't got a moist and smooth dough. Transfer the dough to well – oiled bowl, cover with plastic wrap and leave for 60 – 90 minutes to rise.
2.   Place dough onto a floured surface and carefully deflate. Then, divide the dough evenly into 6 pieces and form each one into a 1½" wide and 12" long log. Transfer them onto a large greased baking sheet. Cover using a kitchen towel and leave for 30 – 45 minutes.
3.   Preheat the oven to 400F.
4.   Brush your bread with beaten egg and sprinkle with sunflower seeds, pepitas, and poppy seeds.
5.   Bake for 25 minutes or longer to get a deeper crust.
6.   Take the baguettes out of the oven and allow to completely cool on a cooling rack.

Wheat Shaft Baguette

SERVINGS: 1 PREP TIME: 20 min. + 2 h. COOK TIME: 35 min.

CARBS – 46 g FAT – 1 g PROTEIN – 8 g CALORIES – 234

Ingredients

- *1½ Tbsp granulated yeast*
- *1½ Tbsp kosher salt*
- *3 cups lukewarm water*
- *6½ cups bread flour, plus more for the work surface and shaping*

Directions

1. Mix the yeast, water, and salt in a large bowl. Add the flour and mix with a stand mixer (paddle attachment). Cover using a kitchen towel and leave for 2 hours to double in size.

2. Next, flour the surface of the dough and cut off a ½ – pound portion. Flour a piece of dough and form a ball: stretch its surface around the bottom while rotating the dough a quarter – turn as you go. Leave the dough for 10 minutes.

3. Form a rectangle of sorts from the ball. Next, using the palms of hands, carefully roll it into a 16" baguette. Save the rest of the unused dough in the fridge. Turn over the baking sheet and line it with parchment paper. Transfer your dough onto it and leave for 40 minutes to rise.

4. Put another baking sheet in the middle of the oven and roasting pan in the bottom of the oven. Preheat it to 450°F.

5. Dust your dough with flour. Cover the blades of your kitchen scissors with oil and cut into the dough crosswise near the top of the baguette shape, at an angle of 25° to the dough and stopping a quarter inch from its bottom. Fold every cut part over to the side while alternating sides with every cut. Repeat to cut the entire loaf.

6. Gently transfer the loaf onto the baking sheet and pour 1 cup of hot water into the pan. Close the oven and bake for 25 – 30 minutes or longer for a deeper color.

7. Remove the baguette from the oven and let it cool completely before serving.

Classic Ciabatta

SERVINGS: 00 PREP TIME: 20 min. + 8 h. COOK TIME: 1 h.

CARBS – 25 g FAT – 1 g PROTEIN – 3 g CALORIES – 131

Ingredients

- *3½ cups unbleached, unbromated white bread flour*
- *1½ tsp fine sea salt*
- *1 tsp instant dry yeast*
- *1½ cups warm water 65°F, + 2 tsp water*
- *1 Tbsp extra – virgin olive oil + extra*

Directions

1.   Mix the yeast, flour, and salt in a large bowl, add half of the water into the mixer bowl (using the dough hook). Add all of the dry ingredients and mix at a low speed. Quickly pour in enough of the rest of the water in a slow stream to get a soft and moist dough. Stop mixing and scrape down the hook and the sides of the bowl with a spatula. Mix for 5 more minutes when you've added all the water.

2.   Next, mix for 4 minutes on a medium – low speed while adding 1 tsp of olive oil. Mix for 1 more minute until oil has been fully incorporated. The dough should be smooth and soft with a moist surface. Cover and leave for 3 hours, with a fold after each hour.

3.   Oil a large bowl with extra olive oil and put your dough into it. Using your hands, pull one edge, fold it to the center and lightly press down. Turn the bowl and repeat for the rest of the edges to form a ball. Turn the ball in the bowl to coat it with oil. Leave the dough for 3 hours, folding each hour.

4.   Flour a work surface well. Dust the top of the dough and place it onto the work surface. Lightly dust all the sides of the dough and let it rest for 30 seconds.

5.   Form a large rectangle from the dough. Put it in a floured couche and cover. Leave for 45 – 60 minutes, but keep an eye on the dough and determine whether it is ready to be baked. With your fingertip, make dents in the center of the dough. If it slowly and evenly disappears, you can bake it.

6.   Put a baking stone on the bottom rack and preheat the oven to 450°F.
7.   Line a bread peel with parchment paper. Transfer the bread to the peel, top side up. Place the dough on the parchment paper onto the middle of the stone. Cover it with a large stainless – steel bowl and close the oven. Bake for 10 minutes then remove the bowl. Bake for 15 more minutes to get a golden ciabatta.
8.   Take out of the oven and put the ciabatta on a cooling rack. Let it cool completely before slicing.

No – Knead Ciabatta

SERVINGS: 1 PREP TIME: 10 min. + 18 h. COOK TIME: 30 min.

CARBS – 12 g FAT – 14 g PROTEIN – 2 g CALORIES – 178

Ingredients
- *4 cups unbleached all – purpose flour*
- *1½ tsp kosher salt*
- *¼ tsp active dry yeast*
- *2 cups water*
- *1 Tbsp olive oil*
- *2 Tbsp cornmeal*

Directions
1. Mix the yeast, flour, and salt in a large bowl. Add the water and mix well, using a rubber spatula. Cover with foil and leave for 18 hours at room temperature.
2. Next, oil a rimmed baking sheet with a brush, dust with cornmeal and set aside.
3. Wipe the work surface with water and line it with a piece of plastic wrap. Flour it to prevent the dough sticking.
4. Place your dough onto the floured plastic wrap. Press and form a long flat loaf from the dough. Next, flip your dough over on the prepared sheet pan using the plastic wrap. Lightly dust the top of the ciabatta with flour and cover with a kitchen towel for 2 hours.
5. Preheat the oven to 425°. Put the rack in the lower third position. When it's preheated, transfer the sheet pan into the oven. Bake for 25 – 30 minutes or more until you get beautiful deep golden crust.
6. Remove from the oven and let the ciabatta to cool completely before slicing on a cooling rack.

Quick Ciabatta

SERVINGS: 2 PREP TIME: 30 min. + 3 h. COOK TIME: 30 min.

CARBS – 14 g FAT – 1 g PROTEIN – 2 g CALORIES – 82

Ingredients

- *4 cups all – purpose flour*
- *2 ¼ tsp active dry yeast*
- *2 ¼ cups warm water*
- *1 tsp salt*
- *¼ tsp sugar*

Directions

1. Mix the yeast, sugar, and water in a mixing bowl and set aside for 5 minutes. Add the flour and salt and mix in a stand mixer with a paddle. You should get almost a pancake batter, only thicker.
2. Let it stand for 15 minutes. Then mix it at a medium – high speed for 6 minutes. Next, switch the paddle to the dough hook and mix for 6 more minutes to make the dough smooth and not sticking to the bowl.
3. Grease another bowl with oil and put the dough inside. Cover using a kitchen towel and leave for 2 hours in a warm place to triple in size. While it's rising, line a baking sheet with parchment paper and then dust it with flour.
4. Place your dough on the center of the baking sheet and flour the top. Divide the dough evenly into two pieces with a bench scraper. Also, use it and wet hand to shape the dough – tuck every irregular part underneath to get two flat logs. The logs should be about 6" apart. Remember that wet dough doesn't hold a definite shape, so you don't need to shape it perfectly.
5. Dust the tops with flour and cover using a kitchen towel for 1 hour to rise.
6. Preheat your oven to 500°F, keeping the baking stone inside for 30 minutes. Place a pan on the bottom rack.
7. Place the loaves on the baking stone by sliding the parchment off the sheet and pour hot water into the pan, close the oven. Bake for 25 minutes or until the bread has a golden – brown color.
8. Remove from the oven and cool for 40 minutes before slicing.

Whole – Wheat Ciabatta

SERVINGS: 1 PREP TIME: 45 min. + overnight COOK TIME: 30 min.

CARBS – 26 g FAT – 1 g PROTEIN – 4 g CALORIES – 135

Ingredients

For the sponge:
- *1 cup warm water*
- *½ cup all – purpose flour*
- *½ cup whole wheat flour*
- *¼ cup rye flour*
- *¼ tsp active dry yeast*

For the final dough:
- *1 cup all – purpose flour*
- *1 cup whole wheat flour*
- *½ cup water at room temperature*
- *2 Tbsp shelled sunflower seeds*
- *1 Tbsp polenta*
- *1 Tbsp ground flax seeds*
- *1 ¾ tsp salt*
- *1 ½ tsp honey*
- *1 tsp all – purpose flour, or as needed*
- *½ tsp cornmeal, or as needed*

Directions

1.	Mix all of the sponge ingredients in a large mixing bowl. Cover with plastic wrap and leave for 5 – 6 hours to double in size.
2.	Then, stir in all the ingredients for the final dough into the bowl with a sponge. Mix for 3 – 4 minutes with a wooden spoon until you get a sticky dough ball. Scrape down all sides of the bowl, cover again with plastic wrap, and leave overnight.

3. Line your baking sheet with parchment and dust it with ½ tsp all – purpose flour and cornmeal.
4. Transfer your dough onto the floured surface and press to deflate the air. Shape into a smooth rectangle loaf. Transfer it onto the prepared baking sheet, lightly dust them and cover with plastic wrap for 1 hour and 30 minutes.
5. Preheat the oven to 450°F. Put a skillet on the bottom rack and pour 1 cup of hot water into it.
6. Lightly mist the top of the loaf and put it into the oven. Bake for 30 – 35 minutes, dampening the top of the bread every 8 minutes.
7. Remove your bread from oven and cool completely on a cooling rack before slicing.

PIZZA AND FOCACCIA
Perfect Pizza Dough

SERVINGS: 2 PREP TIME: 10 min. + 1 h. 30 minutes COOK TIME: 15 min.

CARBS – 17 g FAT – 1 g PROTEIN – 2 g CALORIES – 91

Ingredients
- 1 cup + 1 Tbsp warm water, 110° – 115°F
- 2¼ tsp active dry yeast
- 1 tsp granulated sugar
- 3 cups all – purpose flour
- 1 tsp kosher salt
- 1 Tbsp extra virgin olive oil

Directions
1. Sprinkle the yeast over warm water. Next, sprinkle sugar over the yeast. Leave until the water starts to become frothy. Start it over again if it doesn't.
2. Add the salt and flour to a food processor and pulse for 1 minute. While pulsing, add in the olive oil, then add the yeast mixture with the food processor still running to get a dough ball. You can also use a stand mixer fitted with the dough hook.
3. Grease a large bowl with oil or use cooking spray. Place the dough into this bowl and cover with plastic wrap. Leave for 60 – 90 minutes to double in size.
4. Flour the work surface and transfer your dough onto it. Divide the dough evenly into two dough balls.
5. Use your dough or keep it the fridge for up to 2 days. Let it warm to room temperature for 1 hour before shaping.

No – Knead Pizza Dough

SERVINGS: 2 PREP TIME: 5 min. + 2 h. COOK TIME: 15 min.

CARBS – 18 g FAT – 1 g PROTEIN – 2 g CALORIES – 87

Ingredients
- *4 cups flour*
- *1½ tsp instant yeast*
- *1½ tsp salt*
- *1½ cups lukewarm water*
- *1 tsp olive oil*

Directions
1.   Add the salt, flour, and yeast into the stand mixer bowl fitted with a paddle attachment. Mix for 1 – 2 minutes at a low speed. Pour all of the water into the bowl and mix for 1 – 2 minutes until you get a dough that doesn't stick to the sides
2.   You don't have to knead the dough. It should be soft and sticky without any flour streaks on the surface.
3.   You can also mix the dough with your hands or using a wooden spoon in a large bowl, just follow these steps.
4.   Grease a large mixing bowl with oil. Flour your hands and form a ball from the dough. Transfer it to the greased bowl and turn it a few times to coat it with oil.
5.   Cover with plastic wrap and leave for 2 – 3 hours to double in size.
6.   When the dough has risen, it's ready to use for making pizza. You can put into the fridge for up to 2 days for further use. Remember to let it warm to room temperature for 1 hour before shaping.

Vegan Pizza Dough

SERVINGS: 2 PREP TIME: 15 min. + 2 h. COOK TIME: 10 min.

CARBS – 61 g FAT – 1 g PROTEIN – 9 g CALORIES – 303

Ingredients
- *2½ cups all – purpose flour + more*
- *1 tsp instant yeast*
- *¼ tsp salt*
- *1 tsp olive oil + more*
- *¾ cup water*

Directions
1. Mix the salt, flour, yeast in a large bowl. Then pour in the water and oil. Create a non – sticky and soft dough ball by mixing and kneading it. Add more water if it's crumbly. If it's still sticky, add flour.
2. Coat the ball with olive oil, then cover with a kitchen towel and leave for 2 – 3 hours to double in size.
3. Next, divide the dough evenly into two portions. Bake your pizza now with your favorite toppings now or freeze it for future use.
4. If ready to bake, then gently roll the dough out onto floured parchment paper into two round pizza crusts without much pressure. Stretch it with your hands to get the right shape.
5. Transfer your pizza dough on the parchment paper onto a baking tray.
6. Add toppings and bake the pizza for 10 – 15 minutes in the oven preheated to 480°F until your crust is slightly crispy and golden.

Neapolitan Pizza Crust

SERVINGS: 4 PREP TIME: 30 min. + 2 – 4 days COOK TIME: 15 min.

CARBS – 12 g FAT – 1 g PROTEIN – 2 g CALORIES – 57

Ingredients
- *4 cups bread flour*
- *2 tsp kosher salt*
- *2¼ tsp instant yeast*
- *1½ cups warm water*
- *1 handful cornmeal for pizza peel*

Directions
1. Add the yeast, flour, and salt to a large bowl and mix well to combine. Pour in the water and mix with your hands to fully incorporate it leaving no dry flour on the sides and bottom of the bowl. Cover with plastic wrap and leave for 8 – 12 hours at room temperature.
2. Lightly flour the work surface and transfer your dough onto it. Divide it evenly into 4 balls. Put each ball into a separate zipper – lock freezer bag and refrigerate for 2 – 4 days to rise.
3. Take out of the fridge and shape each portion into a ball. Then cover them with a towel and let them rise for 2 hours before baking.
4. When it's time to bake, set the oven rack to the highest level and put a pizza stone or baking sheet on it. Set to the highest temperature to preheat the oven.
5. Sprinkle the pizza peel with cornmeal and stretch a 8 – 10" circle out of the dough with your hands.
6. The dough is ready to use for making pizza. Remember not to overfill it with topping – this dough can't handle it.

Artisan Margherita Pizza

SERVINGS: 1 PREP TIME: 15 min. + 1 h. COOK TIME: 15 min.

CARBS – 44 g FAT – 17 g PROTEIN – 14 g CALORIES – 388

Ingredients

For the dough:
- 2 ⅓ cups bread flour, plus more for work surfaces
- 1 cup carbonated water
- 1 package quick – rising yeast
- 2 Tbsp extra – virgin olive oil
- 2 ¼ tsp kosher salt, divided

For the sauce:
- ½ can tomatoes, drained
- 1 Tbsp extra – virgin olive oil
- ½ garlic clove, minced
- ½ tsp salt
- 2 125 – g tubs buffalo mozzarella, drained and sliced
- ½ cup grated parmesan
- Few basil leaves

Directions

1. You can use one of the other pizza recipes from this book (see Perfect Pizza Dough or No – Knead Pizza Dough recipes) or follow the below directions. Add the salt, flour, and yeast to a large bowl and mix well with a fork. Pour in the water and oil. Continue mixing until it is well blended. Then, carefully knead the dough on a floured work surface until it starts to come together. Divide it evenly into two pieces and form the balls.

2. Prepare a baking sheet by generously dusting it with flour. Transfer the dough balls onto the sheet and pinch their bottoms. Cover with plastic wrap and leave for 1 hour.

3.   Place your pizza stone on the central oven rack and set to 500°F to preheat the oven.

4.   Meanwhile, make the sauce. Add the garlic, tomatoes, oil, and salt to a food processor and pulse until smooth.

5.   Refrigerate 1 dough ball for future use. Dust a work surface and a large piece of parchment paper with flour. On the work surface, stretch one dough ball into an 11" circle with your hands, leaving the outer edges thicker and place on the paper.

6.   Spread the tomato sauce on the pizza dough, leaving a 1" border and top with mozzarella.

7.   Slide the pizza dough onto the paper onto another inverted baking sheet, and then slide onto the preheated sheet in the oven. Bake for 12 – 13 minutes until the crust is brown and the cheese is golden. Sprinkle the pizza with parmesan and basil leaves before serving.

8.   Serve right from the oven and enjoy a delicious classic Italian pizza.

Chicken Pesto Pizza

SERVINGS: 1 PREP TIME: 15 min. COOK TIME: 25 min.

CARBS – 33 g FAT – 25 g PROTEIN – 25 g CALORIES – 450

Ingredients

- *1 pizza dough (see Perfect Pizza Dough or No – Knead Pizza Dough recipes)*
- *½ cup basil pesto*
- *2 cups shredded mozzarella cheese*
- *1 cup shredded cooked chicken breast*
- *2 large cherry tomatoes, thinly sliced*

Directions

1. If you already have the dough in the fridge, take it out of the fridge and let it warm for 1 hour at room temperature. Lightly dust before shaping.
2. Preheat the oven to 425°F. Use cooking spray to oil a 15x10" pan with sides.
3. Place the dough in the pan to shape. Starting from the center, press the dough into a rectangle (15x10"). Bake for 8 minutes to get a light brown pizza base.
4. Spread the pesto to within ½ an inch of the edge of the crust. Top with 1½ cups of cheese, chicken, and sliced tomatoes. Sprinkle with the rest of the cheese.
5. Bake for 5 minutes or more to get a golden brown crust and melted cheese.
6. Remove from the oven and sprinkle with chopped basil. Serve immediately.

Hawaiian Pizza

SERVINGS: 6 PREP TIME: 1 h. COOK TIME: 10 min.

CARBS – 30 g FAT – 9 g PROTEIN – 11 g CALORIES – 246

Ingredients

- *1 pizza dough (see Perfect Pizza Dough or No – Knead Pizza Dough recipes)*
- *1 cup pineapple, ½ – pieces*
- *¼ sweet onion, thinly sliced*
- *1 Tbsp extra – virgin olive oil*
- *1 pinch fine sea salt*
- *⅓ cup tomato sauce*
- *¼ cup Pecorino Romano cheese, grated*
- *2 ounces cooked ham, sliced*
- *1½ ounces mozzarella cheese, grated*

Directions

1.   If using already made dough, remove your dough ball from the fridge 1 hour before baking the pizza. Place your pizza stone or upside – down rimmed baking sheet on an upper oven rack. Preheat the oven to 550°F for 45 minutes.
2.   Meanwhile, add the onion and pineapple to a cast – iron skillet and toss them with salt and oil. Roast for 10 minutes at 550°F or until they are tender and caramelized. Flour the work surface and place next to it lightly floured wooden peel. Set the oven to broil for 10 minutes before baking the pizza.
3.   Place the dough ball on the floured work surface and coat both sides with flour. Shape the dough with your hands and leave a puffy edge. Put the pizza dough on the peel. Run around the perimeter and work out the kinks.
4.   Spread the sauce over the dough. Add the rest of the ingredients in this order: pecorino, ham, pineapple, onion, and mozzarella.
5.   Switch off the broiler and slide your pizza onto the hot pizza stone. Close the oven door and set to 550°F. Bake for 5 minutes. Then turn on the broiler, and bake for 2 more minutes until the cheese has fully melted and the crust is golden with brown spots.
6.   Remove from the oven and serve immediately.

Pizza Cubano

SERVINGS: 1 PREP TIME: 15 min. COOK TIME: 30 min.

CARBS – 54 g FAT – 13 g PROTEIN – 23 g CALORIES – 413

Ingredients

- *1 pizza dough (see Perfect Pizza Dough or No – Knead Pizza Dough recipes)*
- *2 Tbsp yellow mustard*
- *1 dill pickle, chopped*
- *½ small onion, chopped*
- *1 cup rotisserie chicken, shredded*
- *2 oz. thinly sliced baked ham*
- *½ cup fresh flat – leaf parsley*
- *3 oz. Gruyere cheese, coarsely grated*

Directions

1. If you're going to use the pizza dough from the refrigerator, remove it from the fridge and allow to warm for 1 hour at room temperature. Dust with flour before shaping.
2. Preheat the oven to 475°F. Line one baking sheet with parchment paper.
3. Flour a surface and place the dough onto it. Shape it into a 14" oval and gently transfer it onto the lined baking sheet.
4. Spread mustard onto the crust with, then add the pickle and onion. Top with ham, chicken, parsley, and cheese.
5. Put into the oven and bake for 12 – 15 minutes until the crust has a golden – brown color.
6. Remove from oven and serve immediately.

Extra Meat Pizza

SERVINGS: 1 PREP TIME: 20 min. COOK TIME: 22 min.

CARBS – 53 g FAT – 23 g PROTEIN – 25 g CALORIES – 565

Ingredients

- *1 pizza dough (see Perfect Pizza Dough or No – Knead Pizza Dough recipes)*
- *¾ cup marinara sauce*
- *6 oz. mozzarella cheese*
- *4 oz. sweet Italian sausage meat, cooked*
- *¼ cup olives, sliced (optional)*
- *1 cup mushrooms, sliced*
- *1 small green pepper*
- *3 oz. pepperoni*
- *3 strip crumbled cooked bacon*

Directions

1. Make the dough or use a prepared one if you have it. Let the dough warm for 1 hour before shaping if using it from the fridge.
2. Preheat the oven to 475°F and put a large baking sheet inside.
3. Stretch your pizza dough round into a circle. Place it on a sheet parchment paper, then stretch and press the dough until you get 14" circle with a slight rim.
4. Spread on the sauce and top with mozzarella in one layer. Take out the baking sheet and, holding the parchment, transfer the pizza on the preheated sheet.
5. Then top with mushrooms, pepper, pepperoni, olives, and bacon. Crumble Italian sausage on top.
6. Put into the oven and bake for 22 minutes or until the vegetables are tender.
7. Take out of the oven and serve immediately.

Spicy Pepperoni Pizza

SERVINGS: 1 PREP TIME: 15 min. COOK TIME: 40 min.

CARBS – 52 g FAT – 26 g PROTEIN – 17 g CALORIES – 500

Ingredients

- *1 pizza dough (see Perfect Pizza Dough or No – Knead Pizza Dough recipes)*
- *1 cup marinara sauce*
- *1 Tbsp olive oil*
- *8 oz. mixed mushrooms, sliced*
- *2 cloves garlic, chopped*
- *¼ cup olives, sliced (optional)*
- *2 oz. pepperoni slice*
- *8 oz. mozzarella cheese, shredded*
- *½ cup Parmesan cheese, grated*
- *1 tsp crushed red pepper*
- *2 Tbsp honey*

Directions

1. If you already have the dough in the fridge, take it out from the fridge and let it warm for 1 hour at room temperature. Lightly dust before shaping.
2. Preheat the oven to 475°F. Line a baking sheet with parchment.
3. Transfer your dough onto a floured surface and stretch and press with your hands to get a pizza disk. Transfer it onto the prepared baking sheet.
4. Spread the sauce all over pizza dough, then put into the oven and bake for 10 minutes.
5. Heat oil in a skillet on medium. Add the garlic and mushroom and cook for 5 minutes while stirring.
6. Take out the pizza and spread the mushrooms over it. Then top with pepperoni, olives, and cheese.
7. Bake for 15 – 20 minutes to get nice golden – brown color.
8. Remove and sprinkle with red pepper, then drizzle with a little honey before serving.

No – Knead Focaccia Bread

SERVINGS: 1 PREP TIME: 15 min. + 1 day COOK TIME: 20 min.
CARBS – 29 g FAT – 3 g PROTEIN – 5 g CALORIES – 160

Ingredients

For the dough:
- 1 ¼ cups warm water
- 1 tsp active yeast

- 3 cups all – purpose flour
- 1 tsp salt

For the cooking:
- 1 Tbsp water
- 1 Tbsp olive oil
-

- 1 tsp dry oregano
- ¼ tsp sea salt flakes

Directions

1.   Mix the water and yeast in a bowl. Next, add the flour and salt. Mix until there are no lumps using a wooden spoon. Cover with cling film and leave for 30 minutes.
2.   Spread some olive oil on the work surface and place the batter onto it.
3.   Wet your hands and grab the side of the dough, then stretch and fold it over the top. Repeat for the remaining three sides. Flip the dough upside down. Then, cover it with oiled cling film and let it rest for 30 minutes. Repeat this step 3 more times.
4.   Next, place your dough upside down into a well – oiled bowl. Cover and leave in the fridge for 1 day.
5.   Preheat the oven to 500ºF. Put the rack on the second highest level in the oven. Line a 9x13" pan with a baking sheet. Grease it generously with oil.
6.   Turn the bowl on top of the pan and wait until the dough falls into the pan by itself. Dampen your hands and carefully stretch the dough to fit the pan, trying not to poke the air pockets. Then leave it for 30 minutes.
7.   Before baking make few indentations in the dough with wet hands.
8.   Combine 1 Tbsp water + 1 Tbsp olive oil. Drizzle over the top of the dough, then sprinkle with oregano and sea salt flakes.   Bake for 20 minutes or longer to get golden brown color.
9.   Take out of the oven and let it cool for 30 minutes on a cooling rack before serving.

Rosemary Focaccia Bread

SERVINGS: 1 PREP TIME: 15 min. + 1 h. COOK TIME: 20 min.

CARBS – 26 g FAT – 4 g PROTEIN – 5 g CALORIES – 168

Ingredients
- *1⅓ cups warm water, 110°F*
- *2 tsp sugar*
- *1 package active dry yeast*
- *3½ cups all – purpose flour*
- *¼ cup extra virgin olive oil*
- *2 tsp sea salt*
- *2 sprigs fresh rosemary*

Directions
1.   Pour water into the stand mixer bowl , add the sugar, then mix. Sprinkle the yeast over the water and give it a stir. Let it start to foam (5 – 10 minutes).
2.   Set the mixer with the dough hook to a low speed, and slowly add the flour, oil, and salt. Set to medium – low and mix for 5 minutes. Add in an extra ¼ cup of flour while it is mixing if the dough is too sticky.
3.   Remove the dough from the bowl and form a dough ball with your hands. Grease a mixing bowl with oil and place the ball inside. Cower with a damp towel and leave for 1 hour in a warm place.
4.   Then, place your dough onto a floured work surface. Roll out a large ½" thick rectangle. Cover again and leave for 20 more minutes.
5.   Preheat the oven to 400°F. Line a large baking sheet with parchment paper. Poke deep dents all over the dough surface with your fingers. Drizzle the top evenly with olive oil and sprinkle with rosemary needles and sea salt flakes.
6.   Bake for 20 minutes or longer to get a slightly golden focaccia. Remove the cooked bread from the oven and let it cool completely.

Cranberry and Goat Cheese Focaccia Bread

SERVINGS: 1 PREP TIME: 1 h. 10 min. COOK TIME: 30 min.

CARBS – 32 g FAT – 6 g PROTEIN – 4 g CALORIES – 201

Ingredients

- *1 Tbsp dry active yeast*
- *1 Tbsp sugar*
- *1½ cups warm water 100°F, divided*
- *3¼ cups all – purpose flour*
- *2 tsp kosher salt*
- *2 Tbsp extra virgin olive oil*
- *½ cup halved fresh cranberries*
- *2 Tbsp minced rosemary*
- *2 oz goat cheese, crumbled*
- *¼ cup rosemary oil*
- *2 Tbsp honey*
- *Freshly ground black pepper, to taste*
- *Flaky sea salt, to taste*

For the rosemary oil:
- *1 cup extra virgin olive oil*
- *4 large sprigs rosemary*

Directions

1.   Add the ingredients for the rosemary oil in a medium pan and cook over a medium – high heat for 4 – 5 minutes. Remove from the heat let it cool while making the focaccia.
2.   Combine the yeast, sugar, and ¼ cup of water in a bowl. Let it sit for 5 minutes.
3.   Meanwhile, mix the flour and salt in another large bowl. Add in the rest of the water, oil, and yeast. Stir well to combine.

4. Grease a 9x13" baking pan and place your dough inside. Oil your fingers and spread the dough out to make it reach the corners of the pan. Then, cover with a plastic wrap and leave for 1 hour.
5. Preheat the oven to 375°F.
6. When the dough is ready, grease your hands with oil and make dimples in the dough with your fingers, then sprinkle the rosemary, cranberries, and goat's cheese over the top. Drizzle with honey and the cooled rosemary oil. Season with black pepper and sea salt.
7. Bake for 30 minutes or more for a golden brown focaccia.
8. Take out and let it cool for 20 minutes. Serve with rosemary oil.

Sweet Tomatoes Focaccia

SERVINGS: 1 PREP TIME: 2 h. COOK TIME: 25 min.

CARBS – 46 g FAT – 1 g PROTEIN – 8 g CALORIES – 233

Ingredients

- *8 cups strong bread flour*
- *2 envelopes dry yeast*
- *1 tsp honey*
- *2⅕ cups water (tepid)*
- *1 bulb garlic broken into cloves, skin on*
- *3 Tbsp Extra virgin olive oil*
- *5 sprigs rosemary, leaves picked off*
- *11 ounces cherry tomatoes, sliced*
- *¼ tsp sea salt + extra for mortaring*

Directions

1.   Add the flour to a large mixing bowl and form a well in the center. Add the yeast, honey, and sea salt. Pour in almost all of the water. Mix with a wooden spoon until you get a sticky ball. (If it's dry, add the rest of the water).
2.   Grease a bowl with oil and set aside. Place the focaccia dough onto a floured work surface. Flour your hands and start pulling the dough to you with one hand and pushing it away with the other hand. Continue until you get a smooth, soft dough. Form a ball and then place it into an oiled bowl. Then, cover with a damp towel and leave for 1 hour to rise.
3.   Add the garlic, rosemary, and salt in a mortar and crush with a pestle for a minute. Add the olive oil and stir well.
4.   Grease a 13x9" pan with olive oil.
5.   When your dough has risen, check if it is wobbly by gently pressing it. Place onto a floured work surface then knead to deflate. Place the dough into oiled pan and stretch to fit.
6.   Smear rosemary garlic oil over the dough. Make a lot of dents all over the top with your fingers and spread the tomatoes over it. Leave it for 40 minutes to rise.
7.   Preheat your oven to 425°F. Then bake the bread for 25 minutes, take it out and drizzle with oil before serving.

No – Knead Pistachios Focaccia

SERVINGS: **1** PREP TIME: **15 min. + 1 day** COOK TIME: **25 min.**

CARBS – **32 g** FAT – **5 g** PROTEIN – **5 g** CALORIES – **197**

Ingredients
- *3¼ cups all – purpose or bread flour*
- *1 Tbsp kosher salt*
- *1 tsp instant yeast*
- *1½ cups minus 1 Tbsp water*
- *¼ cup extra – virgin olive oil, divided*
- *4 ounces pitted green olives, sliced*
- *¼ cup roasted pistachios, chopped*
- *2 Tbsp fresh rosemary leaves, chopped*
- *Coarse sea salt, to taste*

Directions
1. Mix the yeast, flour, salt, and water in a large bowl. With a wooden spoon mix until there is no dry flour. Cover using plastic wrap and leave for 1 day to rise.
2. Next, dust the top of the dough with flour and place it onto a floured work surface. Tuck your dough underneath itself while rotating it to form a tight ball.
3. Add half of the olive oil to a 12" cake pan. Place the dough inside and turn few times to coat with oil. Leave it seam – side down and with a flat palm, press the batter all around the skillet, and at the same time flatten it and spread olive oil around the whole bottom and edges of the pan. Cover with plastic wrap and leave for 2 hours. When 1 hour is up, place an oven rack in the middle of the oven and preheat it to 550°F.
4. When the dough is ready the dough should almost fill the pan up to the edge. By pressing the dough with fingertips, fill each corner and pop any large bubbles that appear. Lift up the dough edge and pop every bubble underneath, and repeat with each edge to remove all of the bubbles. Spread the dough evenly around the skillet.

5.   Spread the pistachios and olives over the top of the bread and press them down slightly. Drizzle with oil, salt, and rosemary.

6.   Put the skillet into the oven and bake for 15 – 25 minutes to get a golden – brown top and crispy bottom (check it with a tin spatula while baking). Take out of the oven and allow to cool a little before serving.

Apricot Prosciutto Focaccia

SERVINGS: 1 PREP TIME: 25 min. + 3 h. COOK TIME: 25 min.

CARBS – 21 g FAT – 10 g PROTEIN – 10 g CALORIES – 210

Ingredients

- *2 ¼ cups extra – virgin olive oil + extra*
- *2 pizza dough (see Perfect Pizza Dough or No – Knead Pizza Dough recipes)*
- *3 apricots, pitted and cut into wedges, grilled*
- *3 ounces goat cheese, crumbled*
- *Kosher salt, to taste*
- *Freshly ground black pepper, to taste*
- *4 slices prosciutto torn*
- *1 cup arugula leaves*

Directions

1. Knead the pizza dough to make it smooth and well – combined. Transfer it in a large greased bowl and cover with a tea towel. Leave for 2 hours.
2. Then, lightly grease a 10x15" pizza pan with oil. Put the dough inside and stretch to fit the pan. Cover again and leave for 30 minutes.
3. Preheat the oven to 425°F. Make dents all over the surface of the dough with your fingertips. Drizzle the bread with olive oil and top with goat's cheese, pressing it lightly into the dough. Sprinkle with salt and pepper.
4. Bake for 25 – 30 minutes until it has a golden – brown color. Take out of the oven and let it cool for 15 minutes on a cooling rack.
5. Transfer your focaccia to a cutting board. Cut into 12 pieces and top with arugula, prosciutto, and grilled apricots.

Focaccia Cheese Bread

SERVINGS: 1 PREP TIME: 30 min. COOK TIME: 30 min.

CARBS – 23 g FAT – 10 g PROTEIN – 12 g CALORIES – 281

Ingredients
- 2¾ cups flour
- 1 tsp salt
- 1 tsp sugar
- 1 Tbsp instant yeast
- 1 tsp garlic powder
- ½ tsp thyme
- ½ tsp oregano
- 1 tsp basil
- 1 pinch black pepper
- 1 Tbsp olive oil
- 1 cup hot water
- 2 Tbsp olive oil
- 1 Tbsp parmesan cheese
- 1 – 2 cups grated mozzarella cheese

Directions
1. Mix all of the dry ingredients in a large bowl. Pour in the water and 1 Tbsp olive oil. Mix until it starts to come together.
2. Grease your work surface generously with oil and place the dough onto in. Knead it to get a smooth texture. Cover using kitchen towel and leave for 20 minutes. Preheat the oven to 425˚F.
3. Stretch dough into a ½" thick rectangle on a greased baking sheet. Brush with 2 Tbsp olive oil and spread the cheese all over the top.
4. Bake for 12 minutes or more until the bread has lightly browned.
5. Take out your bread from the oven and serve hot!

PASTRIES AND BISCUITS

Crescent Rolls

SERVINGS: 8 PREP TIME: 25 min. + 2 h. 30 min. COOK TIME: 30 min.

CARBS – 74 g FAT – 42 g PROTEIN – 10 g CALORIES – 721

Ingredients

- 2 (.25 ounce) packages active dry yeast
- ¾ cup warm water 110°F
- ½ cup white sugar
- 1 teaspoon salt
- 2 eggs
- ½ cup butter, room temperature
- 4 cups all – purpose flour
- ¼ cup butter, softened

Directions

1.   Put the yeast and warm water in a bowl together and wait until the yeast dissolves.

2.   Add the sugar, eggs, salt, butter, and 2 cups of flour and beat to get a smooth mixture. Add in the rest of the flour and mix well. Scrape all the dough from the bowl sides and knead it. Cover with a kitchen towel and leave for 1 hour 30 minutes to double in size.

3.   Lightly flour the work surface and punch the dough down. Divide it evenly in half and roll both halves into a 12" circle. Spread circles with butter and cut them into 10 wedges. Roll them up, starting from the wide end. Transfer them with the point underneath on a greased baking sheet. Cover and leave for 1 hour.

4.   Preheat the oven to 400°F. Bake for 12 – 15 minutes until the rolls have a golden – brown color. Take out of the oven and brush the tops with butter while the rolls are hot.

5.   You also can fill them with your favorite toppings or use the dough for other recipes.

Artisan Croissant Dough

SERVINGS: 8 PREP TIME: 10 min. + 1 h. COOK TIME: 15 min.

CARBS – 25 g FAT – 14 g PROTEIN – 4 g CALORIES – 259

Ingredients

- *1 tsp (5 g) dried yeast*
- *½ cup (140 g) water weighed on scales*
- *2 cups (250 g) strong flour*
- *1½ Tbsp (20 g) sugar*
- *⅓ Tbsp (5 g) salt*
- *½ cup (150 g) unsalted butter shaped into a flat block*

Directions

1.   In this recipe, you should use the scales to recreate the exact amount of ingredients that were used. Every gram is important!
2.   Mix the water and yeast in a large bowl until the yeast dissolves. Then, add the rest of the dry ingredients to another bowl and mix well.
3.   Add the dry mixture to the yeast and stir to bring together. Cover with the smaller bowl and leave for 10 minutes.
4.   Next, knead it in the bowl for 10 seconds by bringing the outside edges to the middle. Shape a dough ball.
5.   Cover the dough ball with the bowl and leave to rest for 10 minutes.
6.   Repeat steps 4 and 5 steps and then form a flat square shape (10x5 cm). Put the dough into the fridge overnight.
7.   Take out the dough onto a floured work surface and form a dough ball. Make a cut across halfway down the dough ball and pull its corners to open it into a square.
8.   Put cold butter in the middle of your dough and wrap it around the butter, making sure there is no hole.
9.   Pull it to the edge of the surface, long length to the edge, and start to flatten the butter with a rolling pin.

10. Turn the dough to put the short length at the bottom and roll out to reach the length of the rolling pin. Flip your dough over to check it isn't sticking.

11. Fold the dough length into 3. Place in a plastic bag put into the fridge for 30 minutes

12. Take out the dough onto the floured work surface and repeat steps 9, 10, and 11 twice.

13. Roll the dough out to A4 size, with the long length at the bottom, and then cut to divide it into 4 equal strips. Cut each piece along the diagonal and carefully stretch the dough.

14. At the short end, make a cut and form croissant shape by rolling up the dough while using the corners. Before transferring your croissant onto a baking sheet lined with silicone paper, the end piece should be secured underneath.

15. Proof croissant dough: put it in the oven. Set to 120°F and turn off. Wait for 30 minutes.

16. Next, beat the egg with water and glaze your croissants.

17. Preheat the oven to 480°F and put the croissants inside. Turn down to 410°F and bake for 10 – 15 minutes.

18. Take your bread out of the oven, then let it cool for 20 minutes.

Puff Pastry Dough

SERVINGS: **1** PREP TIME: **20 min.** COOK TIME: **20 min.**

CARBS – **20 g** FAT – **19 g** PROTEIN – **3 g** CALORIES – **256**

Ingredients

- *2 cups all – purpose flour, plus 1 Tbsp*
- *1 tsp salt*
- *⅔ cup ice water*
- *8 ounces unsalted butter, cold*

Directions

1. Mix the flour and salt, then turn it out in a pile onto the work surface. Form a well in the center. Add 1 Tbsp of water into it. Fluff the dough quickly with your fingers, using a scooping motion and keeping them loose. Repeat this process until the flour comes together in pieces and holds when you press on it.
2. Then, press it into a square and wrap in plastic. Refrigerate for 30 minutes.
3. Cut the butter into large pieces and sprinkle 1 tsp flour over them. Pound the butter to soften it with a rolling pin, flouring the pin if needed. Pound the butter flat, then gather it up with a pastry scraper. Repeat this step until you make the butter very pliable, and it doesn't break when folding it over on itself.
4. Next, form a 4x4" butter square and wrap it in plastic. Chill for 10 minutes.
5. Take it out of the fridge and roll it out to a 7" square. Put the butter square on top of the dough at a 90° angle to the dough. Fold the dough corners over the butter to make them meet in the middle. Then, pinch to seal.
6. Place your dough seam side down onto floured work surface and roll out a 12" long and 6" wide rectangle. First, fold the top third to cover the bottom third, then fold the bottom third over the top one.
7. Rotate to make it look like an open book. Roll out the same rectangle and fold it again. Wrap your dough in plastic and let it chill for 30 minutes.
8. Repeat steps 6 and 7 until your dough has been folded 6 times. After this, the dough should be fully smooth and pliable. Let it chill in plastic for 1 hour or overnight before use.
9. Use for other puff pastry recipes or wrap in plastic and freeze for future use.

Apple, Bacon, and Caramelized Onion Turnovers

SERVINGS: **8** PREP TIME: **20** min. COOK TIME: **20** min.

CARBS – **24 g** FAT – **19 g** PROTEIN – **10 g** CALORIES – **324**

Ingredients

- *2 sheets puff pastry (see Puff Pastry Dough recipe)*
- *6 strips bacon, diced*
- *2 yellow onions, sliced thinly*
- *1 apple, diced small*
- *1 egg yolk mixed with one Tbsp warm water*
- *½ tsp cinnamon*
- *½ tsp salt, divided into 3 portions*
- *2 – 3 Tbsp cider vinegar*

Directions

1. Take out the puff pastry from the freezer and let it warm until the dough is ready for baking.
2. Heat a skillet on a medium heat and cook the bacon until it is crispy and golden. Transfer the bacon to a paper towel to drain.
3. Remove the fat from the skillet except for 1 Tbsp of it. Add the salt and sliced onion. Cook for 30 minutes on a low – medium setting until it's soft and caramelized.
4. When the onions are cooked, add the apple and salt. Cook for 5 – 10 minutes to make apples soft but firm in the center. Add the cinnamon and salt. Scrape the bottom and add the vinegar. Let it bubble until fully evaporated, then remove the pan from the heat. Put the bacon and onion mixture in a bowl together and mix well.
5. Preheat the oven to 400°F. Line two sheet pans with parchment paper.
6. Lightly dust the work surface and unfold the puff pastry on top. Flatten any ridges with a rolling pin. Divide each dough sheet evenly into 4 square pieces.
7. Put two spoonfuls of the onion – bacon mixture in the center of each piece. Brush the edge with the yolk and fold your squares over into triangles. Make a few vents on the top with a paring knife and brush each turnover with egg yolk. Place on the baking sheets, saving some space between them.
8. Put in the oven for 20 – 25 minutes until they are toasted and the tops are golden.
9. Take out of the oven and allow to cool for 10 minutes, then serve and enjoy.

Flaky Rosemary Biscuits

SERVINGS: 10 PREP TIME: 15 min. COOK TIME: 15 min.

CARBS – 51 g FAT – 19 g PROTEIN – 7 g CALORIES – 390

Ingredients
- *2½ cups flour + 2 Tbsp*
- *½ tsp salt*
- *2½ tsp baking powder*
- *½ cup butter, chilled and grated*
- *1 tsp fresh rosemary, chopped*
- *1 cup cold buttermilk*
- *2 Tbsp butter for the pan and for finishing*

Directions
1. Preheat the oven to 475 degrees.
2. Mix the flour, baking powder, salt in a large bowl. Add the grated butter and give it a stir. Form a crater.
3. Add the rosemary to the buttermilk. Pour the rosemary buttermilk into a crater and mix to form a ball.
4. Place the ball on a floured work surface. Roll out a ¾" thick rectangle using a rolling pin. Fold to form a smaller rectangle and repeat 4 times.
5. When it's done, roll the dough until ¾" thick and cut using 2" biscuit cutter. Use the scraps and repeat this step to roll out additional biscuits. You should get 10 buttermilk biscuits.
6. Transfer them onto a buttered glass pan and bake for 15 minutes until the biscuits have a golden – brown color.
7. Take out of the oven and brush the biscuits with butter and sprinkle with salt before serving.

Gluten – Free Buttermilk Biscuits

SERVINGS: **12** PREP TIME: **30 min.** COOK TIME: **20 min.**

CARBS – **17 g** FAT – **7 g** PROTEIN – **3 g** CALORIES – **143**

Ingredients

- *2 cups gluten – free all – purpose flour*
- *½ tsp xanthan gum*
- *1 Tbsp gluten – free baking powder*
- *1 tsp salt*
- *2 Tbsp granulated sugar*
- *1 cup buttermilk*
- *6 Tbsp unsalted butter dairy – free*
- *1 large egg egg – free*
- *2 Tbsp gluten – free all – purpose flour*

Directions

1. Preheat the oven to 450° F.
2. Combine the gluten – free flour, baking powder, salt and sugar in a large bowl and stir to combine all of the ingredients.
3. Cut the butter into small pieces and put into the freezer for 10 minutes.
4. Cut the butter into the flour mixture using a pastry cutter to get pea – size pieces.
5. Add the buttermilk and whisked egg. Mix to make dough start to come together.
6. It should be sticky and soft. Remember, you don't need to roll out the dough.
7. Flour a large piece of parchment paper. Put the dough onto it and dust top with flour. Fold it over on itself twice.
8. Form an exactly 7" in diameter and 1" thick dough round using your hands.
9. Cut out the biscuits with a 2" biscuit cutter. DO NOT twist the cutter while cutting! Reform the scraps to cut out more biscuits. You should get 12 biscuits.
10. Transfer the biscuits onto a large greased baking sheet.
11. Preheat the oven to 450°F and bake for 15 – 20 minutes to get golden brown biscuits.
12. Take out and serve hot with butter on top.

Fruit Almond Cruffins

SERVINGS: 6 PREP TIME: 40 min. COOK TIME: 20 min.

CARBS – 53 g FAT – 24 g PROTEIN – 8 g CALORIES – 477

Ingredients
- ½ cup softened unsalted butter, + extra for greasing
- ½ cup icing sugar
- 1 large free – range egg, beaten
- 1 cup ground almonds
- 2 Tbsp plain flour + extra to dust
- 2 x 350g croissant dough (see *Artisan Croissant Dough* recipe)
- 1⅓ cups dried apricots, chopped
- 100g raisins
- 1 tsp ground cinnamon
- ½ cup apricot jam
- 1 Tbsp icing sugar for dusting

Directions
1.   Preheat the oven to 360°F. Grease a 12 – portion muffin tin with butter.
2.   To make the frangipane, beat the icing sugar and butter in a bowl to get a creamy and pale mixture. Then, slowly beat in an egg. Fold in the plain and almond flour. Set it aside.
3.   Unroll the croissant dough onto a floured work surface. Cut 6 equal rectangles from the croissant dough.
4.   Divide the frangipane into 6 filling portions and spread it among the pieces, leaving 1 cm around edges. Sprinkle with fruit and season with cinnamon.
5.   Beginning with a long edge, tightly roll each rectangle up like a swiss roll. Cut each roll in half lengthways and place every piece cut – side up on the floured work surface. Roll each piece up into a rose – shaped spiral, cut – side up, and transfer into the muffin tin. Brush the tops with apricot jam.
6.   Bake for 17 – 20 minutes until golden and puffed.
7.   Take out of the oven and let them cool a little. Brush with more apricot jam and serve.

Cherry Turnovers

SERVINGS: 4 PREP TIME: 20 min. COOK TIME: 20 min.

CARBS – 56 g FAT – 12 g PROTEIN – 4 g CALORIES – 359

Ingredients

- *8 ounces crescent rolls dough (see Crescent Rolls recipe)*
- *1 cup cherry pie filling*
- *½ cup confectioners' sugar*
- *1 – 2 Tbsp milk*

For the filling:
- *In 4 cups pitted tart red cherries*
- *1 cup white sugar*
- *¼ cup cornstarch*

Directions

1. Add the cherries into a small saucepan, close the lid, and heat over a medium heat. Once the cherries have started to release their juice simmer for 10 – 15 minutes while stirring.
2. Whisk the cornstarch and sugar in a bowl and pour it into the saucepan. Mix to combine well. Simmer for 2 – 3 minutes until it has thickened.
3. Remove from the heat and allow to cool completely before use.
4. Preheat the oven to 375°. Lightly dust the work surface and unroll the crescent dough.
5. Line a baking sheet with a piece pf parchment paper.
6. Cut it into four squares and transfer it onto the prepared baking sheet. Place ¼ cup pie filling on one half of each square. Fold the dough over the filling to form a triangle, then seal edges by pinching them with a fork.
7. Put into the oven and bake for 10 – 12 minutes until golden. Take out of the oven and let them slightly cool.
8. Add the confectioners' sugar to a bowl and enough milk to get a drizzling mixture. Drizzle over the warm turnovers and serve.

Pastry Cinnamon Rolls

SERVINGS: **16** PREP TIME: **10 min.** COOK TIME: **20 min.**

CARBS – **26 g** FAT – **11 g** PROTEIN – **2 g** CALORIES – **218**

Ingredients
- *2 sheets puff pastry (see Puff Pastry Dough recipe), thawed*
- *½ cup brown sugar, divided*
- *Ground cinnamon to taste*
- *Flour for dusting*

For the icing:
- *¾ cup powdered sugar*
- *½ tsp vanilla*
- *1 Tbsp half & half*

Directions
1. Preheat the oven to 400°F. Then, line a baking sheet with parchment paper.
2. Flour your work countertop and put the dough sheet onto it. Spread half of the brown sugar over the pastry in a thin layer and lightly press down. Season with cinnamon to taste and roll the dough up. Cut it into 8 equal pieces, then transfer them onto the prepared baking sheet. Repeat with the remaining dough.
3. Put into the oven and bake for 15 – 20 minutes until puffed up.
4. Mix all of the ingredients for the icing in a bowl until slightly thick. Adjust the thickness with powdered sugar if too runny or with half & half if too thick.
5. Take the rolls out of the oven and allow to cool for 10 minutes. Drizzle the warm rolls with icing and serve.

Homemade Soft Pretzel

SERVINGS: 8 PREP TIME: 20 min. COOK TIME: 10 min.

CARBS – 31 g FAT – 6 g PROTEIN – 5 g CALORIES – 197

Ingredients

For the dough:

- 2 ¼ tsp instant quick rise yeast
- 1 cup warm water 110°F
- 1 tsp sugar
- 2.5 cup all – purpose flour
- ½ tsp sea salt

For the topping:

- ½ cup warm water
- 1 Tbsp baking soda
- Vegetable oil for greasing the sheet pan
- Coarse sea salt for sprinkling
- 3 Tbsp unsalted butter melted

Directions

1. Add the yeast, water, and sugar to a stand mixer bowl and leave for 10 minutes to foam. Add in the flour and salt. Take off the dough hook and mix it by hand to combine, then fit the dough hook and knead for 5 minutes on a medium – low speed. The dough should become soft and smooth, and shouldn't stick to the touch.
2. Cover and leave for 30 minutes.
3. Preheat the oven to 450°F and grease a baking sheet with oil.
4. Oil your work surface and place the dough onto it. Cut it into 8 equal pieces.
5. Whisk warm water and baking soda in a bowl. Heat for 1 minute in the microwave. It won't dissolve completely.
6. Roll the pieces of dough into a long rope, and then shape into a pretzel. Dip the pretzels into the soda wash and transfer onto the prepared sheet. Sprinkle the tops with coarse salt, and leave for 10 minutes to rest.
7. Bake for 10 minutes until they are golden brown.
8. Remove from the oven and brush with melted butter. Serve and enjoy!

Sweet Ricotta Pastries

SERVINGS: 12 PREP TIME: 1 h. 15 min. COOK TIME: 1 h. 15 min.

CARBS – 43 g FAT – 7 g PROTEIN – 11 g CALORIES – 290

Ingredients

For the filling:
- ½ cup whole milk
- 2 (3 – by 1 – inch) strips orange zest
- 1 large egg yolk
- 3 Tbsp sugar
- 1 Tbsp cornstarch
- 1 pinch of salt
- ½ tsp pure vanilla extract
- ½ pound fresh ricotta
- ¾ tsp orange – flower water
- 2 Tbsp candied citron, finely chopped

For the pastry:
- 2¼ cups all – purpose flour
- 2 sticks cold unsalted butter
- 6 Tbsp sugar
- ½ tsp salt
- ½ tsp grated orange zest
- 2 large egg yolks
- 2 Tbsp cold water
- 1 large egg + 1 Tbsp water, beaten

Directions

1.   Add the milk and zest to a small saucepan, let it simmer for 2 – 3 minutes and remove from the heat. Whisk the sugar, yolk, cornstarch, and salt in a bowl. Add in the milk, whisk together and pour the mixture into a saucepan.

2.   Let it boil on a medium heat, then cook for 1 minute while whisking. Add the vanilla and stir, then transfer the filling to a clean bowl and let it cool for 1 hour, covered with parchment paper. Remove the zest.

3.   Add the ricotta to a food processor and pulse until smooth. Add the custard and whisk together. Stir in the citron and orange – flower water. Chill before using.

4.   Add the flour, salt, and sugar to a clean food processor, and pulse until well – combined. Add the butter zest and pulse until it looks like coarse meal with pea – size butter lumps. Add the water and yolks, pulse to incorporate until the dough forms large clumps.

5.   Transfer it onto a floured surface and divide evenly into 4 portions. To distribute the fat, smear each piece 1 – 2 times in a forward motion with your hands. Using a pastry scraper, gather the dough together and form a ball. Divide it evenly into 10 – 12 portions. Flour a rolling pin and roll out each piece into a square.

6.   Arrange the squares among the greased muffin cups and leave the flaps out. Fill each square with the filling and close the flaps.

7.   Brush the flaps with the egg wash. Put into the oven and bake for 25 – 30 minutes.

8.   Take out of the oven and let it cool for 10 minutes. Remove the pastries from the muffin cups and cool completely.

Sporcamuss Pastries

SERVINGS: 16 PREP TIME: 10 min. COOK TIME: 40 min.

CARBS – 20 g FAT – 6 g PROTEIN – 3 g CALORIES – 230

Ingredients

- *1 roll puff pastry (see Puff Pastry Dough recipe)*

For the pastry cream:

- *¾ cup Milk*
- *¾ cup Cream*
- *4 Egg yolks*
- *½ cup Sugar*
- *½ tsp Vanilla*
- *2½ Tbsp All – purpose flour*
- *Confectioners' sugar*

Directions

1. Put the cream and milk in a medium pot together and heat over low heat. Do not boil and remove from the heat. Cool until just warm.
2. In another pot whisk the yolks and sugar. Add the flour and vanilla, and whisk again. Pour in the cream mixture and heat the pot over a low heat. Simmer and whisk the cream until it has thickened.
3. Transfer the cream into a glass bowl, cover with plastic wrap, and leave for 20 minutes. Then, put in the fridge for 3 hours.
4. Preheat the oven to 350°F.
5. Slice the puff pastry dough into 16 equal squares. Using a fork pierce each piece few times. Sprinkle sugar on the top.
6. Bake for 20 minutes until the squares are golden and puffed up. Remove from the oven and let them cool.
7. Cut each square in half to get a top and bottom. Fill a piping bag with the prepared cream and fill 16 square bottoms. Close each filled bottom with a top. Sprinkle with powdered sugar before serving.

Onion, Spinach, and Cheese Turnovers

SERVINGS: 9 PREP TIME: 25 min. COOK TIME: 25 min.

CARBS – 50 g FAT – 2 g PROTEIN – 10 g CALORIES – 405

Ingredients

- *1 ball puff pastry dough (see Puff Pastry dough recipe)*
- *2 Tbsp extra virgin olive oil*
- *1 yellow onion, sliced*
- *1 tsp honey, plus more for serving*
- *Kosher salt and pepper, to taste*
- *1 garlic clove, minced*
- *1 Tbsp fresh thyme leaves*
- *¼ tsp freshly grated nutmeg*
- *1 tsp crushed red pepper*
- *1 bunch fresh spinach, chopped*
- *1 cup cheddar cheese, shredded*
- *1 cup Havarti cheese, shredded*
- *1 egg, beaten*
- *¼ cup toasted sesame seeds*

Directions

1. Preheat the oven to 375°F. Line a baking sheet with parchment paper.
2. Preheat a skillet and pour in the olive oil over medium – high heat. Add the onions and honey. Cook for 5 minutes, stirring. Then, season with salt and pepper and cook for 5 – 10 more minutes to caramelize the onions. Add the garlic, nutmeg, red pepper, and thyme, cook for 1 minute. Remove skillet from the heat and in spinach, cheddar, Havarti cheese. Stir well to combine.
3. Place the dough onto the floured work surface. Roll the sheets out and stretch easily. Cut both sheets into 9 equal squares. Divide the filling among half of squares, leaving an empty space a ¼" around the edges. Brush the edges with egg. Close each square with the rest of the squares and seal by crimping with your fingertips.
4. Transfer them onto a prepared baking sheet and brush with beaten egg on top. Bake for 20 – 25 minutes to get a golden – brown pastry.
5. Take out from the oven, drizzle with honey (optional), sprinkle with sesame seeds and serve.

French Apple Tart

SERVINGS: 8 PREP TIME: 30 min. COOK TIME: 1 h.

CARBS – 49 g FAT – 21 g PROTEIN – 4 g CALORIES – 392

Ingredients

For the crust:
- *1 – ½ cups all – purpose flour*
- *½ tsp salt*
- *2 Tbsp granulated sugar*
- *1 – ½ sticks (12 Tbsp) very cold unsalted butter, cut into ½ – inch pieces*
- *¼ cup very cold water*

For the filling:
- *1 – ¾ lbs. baking apples, peeled and cored, cut into 4 cups of 1/8" thick slices*
- *⅓ cup sugar*
- *1 tsp vanilla extract*
- *1 tsp cinnamon*
- *2 Tbsp unsalted butter, melted*
- *⅛ tsp salt*

For the filling:
- *1 Tbsp all – purpose flour*
- *1 egg, beaten*
- *2 Tbsp turbinado sugar*
- *1 Tbsp apricot jelly or jam, for glaze*

Directions

1.   Line a baking sheet with parchment paper. Fit your food processor with a steel blade and add the flour, salt and sugar to it. Pulse to combine. Add the butter and pulse for 5 seconds until the butter is pea – size. Sprinkle ice water over the butter mixture and process for 5 more seconds until crumbly and moist.

2. Transfer your dough onto a floured work surface and knead into a cohesive ball. Shape into a disk by patting it. Flour the work surface and dough. Roll the dough into 8 – 10" in diameter with a rolling pin. Transfer it onto the prepared sheet and refrigerate.

3. Add all of the ingredients for the filling to a large bowl and toss well to combine.

4. Take the dough out of fridge and slide the parchment onto a clean work surface. Roll the dough, on the parchment paper, into a 14" circle and 1/8" thick. Return the parchment and dough to the baking sheet – the dough will curve up the pan lip.

5. Sprinkle the dough evenly with flour. Arrange the apple slices to within 3" of the edge in overlapping concentric circles. Fold the dough edges over the apple slices in a free – form manner, working your way around and making pleats.

6. Brush the pleats evenly with beaten egg. Sprinkle 1 Tbsp turbinado sugar over the crust and 1 Tbsp over the apples. Let it cool for 15 – 20 minutes in the fridge.

7. Meanwhile, preheat the oven to 350°F and put the oven rack in the middle.

8. Bake for 55 – 65 minutes to get tender apples and a cooked golden crust. Take out the pan and place it on a cooling rack.

9. In a small saucepan, mix jam with 1 – ½ tsp of water. Heat over a low – medium heat and then reduce to simmer for 3 – 4 minutes. Brush the apples with syrup.

10. Carefully transfer your tart onto a serving plate, slice, and serve warm.

Cream Peach Pie

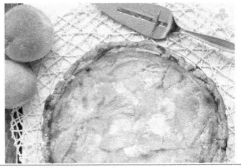

SERVINGS: 8 PREP TIME: 25 min. COOK TIME: 45 min.

CARBS – 40 g FAT – 16 g PROTEIN – 2 g CALORIES – 305

Ingredients

For the pie shell:
- 2 cups all – purpose flour
- ¾ tsp kosher salt
- ½ tsp baking powder
- 11 Tbsp unsalted butter
- 5 – 7 Tbsp cool water

For the filling:
- 4 – 6 ripe peaches
- 1 cup sugar
- 3 Tbsp cornstarch
- 1 pinch of kosher salt
- 1 cup heavy cream
- 1 tsp vanilla

Directions

1. Mix the flour, kosher salt, and baking powder in a medium bowl. Slice the butter into pieces and cut it into flour mixture with a pastry blender to obtain a coarse meal texture.

2. Sprinkle cool water over the flour, mixing it with a fork until the dough comes together. Add additional water until the dough is not sticky. Form two balls from the dough. Let it rest for 15 minutes.

3. Flour the work surface and rolling pin. Take one ball and evenly roll it from the center to the edge, to make it ⅛" thick. Trim it to an even 12" circle.

4. With a rolling pin gently transfer your dough to 9" pie pan. Center and pull the pastry to the bottom. Fold 1" of overhanging dough backwards and form a rim by

sealing it. With your thumb and index finger from one hand and a knuckle from the other, crimp the crust edges.

5.   Repeat this process for the second dough ball (you would need to double the amount of filling) or freeze for later use.

6.   Preheat the oven to 450°F.

7.   Boil water in a large pot. Then boil each peach for 2 minutes (water should cover it) and then remove the skin with sharp knife and your fingers. Cut the peaches in half, remove the pits, and cut into quarters. Arrange the peaches over the pie shell to fill it.

8.   Mix the cornstarch, sugar, and salt in a bowl. Pour in the heavy cream and add the vanilla, mix thoroughly until smooth. Pour it over the peaches.

9.   Preheat the oven to 450°F. Bake for 15 minutes, then reduce to 325°F and bake for 30 – 35 more minutes.

10. Take out of the oven and cool for 1 hour. Put in the fridge overnight to make the custard thicker, and then serve.

Caramel Apple Pie

SERVINGS: 8 PREP TIME: 1 h. COOK TIME: 1h.

CARBS – 87 g FAT – 29 g PROTEIN – 8 g CALORIES – 642

Ingredients

- 2 ½ pounds cooking apples, thinly sliced
- ¼ cup all – purpose flour
- ¼ cup granulated sugar
- ½ tsp ground cinnamon
- 1 egg, lightly beaten
- 1 Tbsp whipping cream
- 1 Tbsp coarse sugar

For the oat pastry:

- 2 cups flour
- ½ cup quick – cooking oats
- 1 tsp salt
- ⅓ cup butter, cut up
- ⅓ cup shortening
- ⅓ – ½ cup ice water
- 2 cup flour

For the caramel sauce:

- 1 package vanilla caramels, unwrapped
- ½ cup whipping cream
- 1 tsp sea salt

Directions

1. To make the oat pastry, mix the oats, flour and salt in a bowl. Use a pastry blender to cut your butter into the mixture (it should be pea – size). Drizzle 1 Tbsp of ice water over the mixture and toss it using a fork. Pull the moistened dough to one side of the bowl. Do the same again, until the dough is fully moist. Form the dough into a ball. Divide it into three equal portions.

2. Meanwhile, add the ingredients for the sauce to a small saucepan. Heat over a medium – low heat and stir until the mixture is melted and smooth.

3. Place one dough on floured work surface and slightly flatten it with your hands. Roll it from the center to the edge into 12" circle. Using a rolling pin, transfer your pastry into a 9" pie form. Ease it to fit into the pie plate, but don't stretch it. Trim any overhanging dough.

4. Add the apple slices to a large bowl. Mix ¼ cup flour, cinnamon, and granulated sugar in another bowl. Sprinkle this mixture over the apples and toss well to coat.

5. Place ⅓ of the filling in the pie shell. Drizzle 2 Tbsp of sauce over the apples. Repeat the layers until there are no apples left.

6. Preheat the oven to 375°F. Whisk the egg and whipping cream in a small bowl. Brush the edge with the egg mixture. Sprinkle the top with coarse sugar.

7. Cover the edge with foil and transfer the pie into the oven. Bake for 30 minutes, then, remove the foil and bake for 25 – 35 minutes to get golden top and bubbly filling.

8. Take out of the oven and cool completely before serving.

CPSIA information can be obtained
at www.ICGtesting.com
Printed in the USA
BVHW050437140521
607269BV00004B/687

9 781649 844903